O9-BUD-824

"James Martin is one of the most important voices in Christian spirituality today and Jon Sweeney's story of his life and his work will, I promise, make you want to be a better person. We need to define what Christian discipleship means in the present moment. This book will help you do that."

—Ronald Rolheiser, author of *The Holy Longing* and *Domestic Monastery*

"Here's what I can't help but love about Jim Martin: his refreshing humanness, his God-help-us-all humor, his faith in Christ, so grounded, so full of search and questioning, so opposite of resting on your 'spiritual laurels,' so honest, so alive and unfurling. And his courage. Father Jim's love for the Church impels him to engage in on-going dialogue about dignity for LGBTQ persons who suffer because of ignorance and prejudice. Courage, Jim. I've stayed in dialogue with my fellow Catholics about the death penalty for 30-plus years. When you love your church, you stay in dialogue."

—Sister Helen Prejean, CSJ, author of *Dead Man Walking* and *The Death of Innocents*

"Jon M. Sweeney has composed a detailed, fascinating portrait of one of our great spiritual leaders, James Martin. From a not very religious family and after a stint on Wall Street, Martin heard the unlikely call to the Jesuits. That this led to his blossoming into a best-selling author and a controversial spokesperson for welcoming LGBTQI+ persons to the Church is a tale woven with marvels. Sweeney's fastidious research and elegant prose make this a page-turner I read with relish and finished with regret. It's a gift to nonbelievers as well as Catholics, lapsed and devout."

—Mary Karr, poet and memoirist, author of *The New York Times* best sellers *The Liars' Club*, *Cherry*, and *Lit*

People of God

Remarkable Lives, Heroes of Faith

People of God is a series of inspiring biographies for the general reader. Each volume offers a compelling and honest narrative of the life of an important twentieth- or twenty-first-century Catholic. Some living and some now deceased, each of these women and men has known challenges and weaknesses familiar to most of us but responded to them in ways that call us to our own forms of heroism. Each offers a credible and concrete witness of faith, hope, and love to people of our own day.

More titles to follow . . .

James Martin, SJ

In the Company of Jesus

Jon M. Sweeney

LITURGICAL PRESS
Collegeville, Minnesota

www.litpress.org

Cover design by Red+Company. Cover illustration by Philip Bannister.

© 2020 by Jon M. Sweeney
Published by Liturgical Press, Collegeville, Minnesota. All rights reserved.
No part of this book may be used or reproduced in any manner what-soever, except brief quotations in reviews, without written permission of Liturgical Press, Saint John's Abbey, PO Box 7500, Collegeville, MN 56321-7500. Printed in the United States of America.

1   2   3   4   5   6   7   8   9

Library of Congress Control Number: 2019946171

ISBN 978-0-8146-4417-1   978-0-8146-4442-3 (e-book)

For my parents,
Mark and Janet Sweeney

Contents

Prologue

Those who knew James Martin as a child and teenager in the suburbs of Philadelphia would never have imagined he would become a Jesuit and a priest. A success, yes, but a religious one? They might have envisioned their imaginative, fun-loving, thoughtful, but not-too-serious friend growing up to become a television, media, and film personality. He was articulate and winsome from an early age. But one of the two or three most recognized priests in the United States? Not a chance. They certainly would not have been able to see a future in which their Jim became a lightning rod for "traditionalist" Roman Catholics who viewed themselves at odds with the Holy See in the second decade of the twenty-first century.

Yet the ways that God invites people to "become who they are," to quote the title of one of Jim's books, are sometimes hard to imagine. This happens in a variety of ways: sometimes through a series of seeming coincidences, sometimes through longings and desires that are hard to understand, sometimes through a chance conversation with a friend. For Jim, the course of his vocation from a somewhat dreamy child to an extroverted adolescent to a hardworking corporate executive and finally to a Jesuit priest came mainly through a book that he chanced upon after seeing a television show. But that's too simplistic an explanation.

In truth, the seeds of his vocation and his later accomplishments can be seen all throughout his life, a life that many people are now coming to know and one that this book invites you to discover.

Basic Chronology

1960   Born in Philadelphia, December 29. Family lives in an apartment in the Germantown section of Philadelphia. Later that year, they move to Plymouth Meeting, a suburb of Philadelphia, where Martin resides for seventeen years, attending elementary school, junior high school, and high school there.

1978   Graduates Plymouth-Whitemarsh High School. In August, at the age of seventeen, enrolls at the University of Pennsylvania's Wharton School of Business.

1982   Graduates college. Moves to an apartment in Manhattan and begins working for General Electric in Midtown. Moves two years later to Queens and then, in 1986, to Stamford, Connecticut, with GE Capital. Promoted to Specialist–Corporate Financial Management Development, he stays at GE until summer 1988.

1986   His parents separate. He begins to consider the direction of his life and then a religious vocation.

1988   August 15, accepted into the Society of Jesus. Thirteen days later, enters Arrupe House, the Jesuit novitiate in Jamaica Plain, Massachusetts. Fall, works in a hospital for seriously ill patients in Cambridge, Massachusetts.

1989   February, sent to Kingston, Jamaica, as a Jesuit novice, to work among the poor with the Missionaries of Charity at Our Lady Queen of Peace hospice. June, completes the Spiritual Exercises of St. Ignatius at Eastern Point Retreat House in Gloucester, Massachusetts.

1990   August, pronounces First Vows (poverty, chastity, and obedience) at the completion of his novitiate. Moves to Arrupe House at Loyola University Chicago for two years of philosophy studies, the second stage of his Jesuit formation. Works with street-gang members and homeless men and women. Begins writing.

1992   Early August, arrives in Nairobi, Kenya, on Jesuit mission for his regency. Works with the Jesuit Refugee Service/East Africa for two years, helping refugees start small businesses. Publishes his first article in *National Jesuit News*, in December, and begins to desire authorship.

1993   March–May, writes *In Good Company*, a memoir about working at GE and joining the Jesuits while in Kenya sick with mononucleosis. A memoir article first appears in *The Pennsylvania Gazette*, his college alumni magazine; the book wouldn't be published until 2000. August, cofounds the Mikono Centre, a shop marketing refugee handicrafts in Nairobi.

1995   Briefly moves to America House, New York City, to complete his regency, then to Cambridge, Massachusetts, to begin theology studies at Weston Jesuit School of Theology.

1997 May, first book published: *How Can I Find God? The Famous and the Not-So-Famous Consider the Quintessential Question.*

1998 Ordained a deacon. After completing theology studies, missioned to work at *America* magazine, New York City, where he remains to this day. Also works for one year as a deacon at the Church of St. Ignatius Loyola in New York.

1999 June 12, ordained a priest in Chestnut Hill, Massachusetts, and celebrates First Mass, at the Church of St. Ignatius Loyola in New York City. January, *This Our Exile*, about his work with East African refugees, published.

2000 *In Good Company* published, and Martin receives early taste of national publicity.

2006 *My Life with the Saints*, another spiritual memoir, published March 1. It becomes his first bestseller, with sales of fifty thousand copies in the first twenty-two months; one hundred thousand in forty-eight months.

2007–
2008 Summers, completes his tertianship, the final stage of Jesuit formation; makes the Spiritual Exercises for the second time at the tertianship program in Culver City, California.

2009 November 1, pronounces his Final Vows at the Church of St. Ignatius Loyola, New York City, on the

Feast of All Saints, ten years after being ordained a priest, and twenty-one years after entering the Jesuits.

2010   March 28, *The Jesuit Guide to (Almost) Everything* hits the *New York Times* Best Sellers list. The *Times* editors describe it: "A priest explains the easily applied traditional wisdom that Jesuits use to help other people in their daily lives."

2011   First pilgrimage to the Holy Land, as part of research for his next book.

2014   *Jesus: A Pilgrimage* published in March, becomes a *New York Times* Best Seller.

2015   A first novel, *The Abbey: A Story of Discovery*, published in October. It began as a dream.

2017   The first edition of *Building a Bridge: How the Catholic Church and the LGBT Community Can Enter into a Relationship of Respect, Compassion, and Sensitivity* leads him into a maelstrom of both praise and backlash from fellow Catholics that lasts several years.

2019   Continues to give frequent talks on the importance of welcoming LGBT Catholics—"the most marginalized people in the Church today." Finishes *Learning to Pray*.

2020   Working on a book about Lazarus. Continues to work at America Media.

CHAPTER ONE

Plymouth Meeting, Wharton, General Electric

The house Jimmy Martin grew up in, at 107 Kings Road in Plymouth Meeting, Pennsylvania, looks as ordinary as any suburban dwelling on a quiet neighborhood street. Its 1,600 square feet, split-level, three bedrooms, one-and-a-half baths, were built in the late 1950s. Situated on a small lot with neighbors on either side, it remained unchanged throughout young Jim's life. His mother would not sell it until 2012.

Jim was born at Hahnemann Hospital in Philadelphia on December 29, 1960. His only sibling, Carolyn, was born three years later. Jim was named for his father, who was married to Eleanor, Jim's mom. Both parents were Philadelphia natives.

James Sr. worked in marketing for Wyeth Pharmaceuticals in Radnor, Pennsylvania, and then for Rorer Pharmaceuticals. In his fifties, he lost his job and for years struggled in less satisfying work. Eleanor was both a homemaker and a substitute French teacher in Jim's school district. Before

1

marrying James, she had worked in downtown Philadelphia as a secretary and translator.

Jim's dad was hardworking and taciturn. He had lost both his parents at an early age (first his father, then mother), and Jim sometimes wondered if James had a more difficult time as a parent as a result of this. But James was a typical 1960s father by most accounts; responsibility, hard work at the office, and breadwinning were his primary intentions. He also was often away on lengthy business trips, with both national and international travel.

Jim's dad was also a storyteller and loved a good joke, at times laughing so hard he'd have trouble catching his breath. He was a devout Philadelphia sports fan. One of Jim's childhood memories has the family attending a performance at the old Academy of Music in Philadelphia, home of the Philadelphia Orchestra. A World Series or Stanley Cup game was happening at the time, and his father was determined not to miss it, so he had earphones connected to a transistor radio while at the concert. During a quiet orchestral moment James leapt from his seat and yelled "Score!"[1]

Jim's mother was, like her husband, an intelligent, humorous, and well-read college graduate (his father went to the University of Pennsylvania, his mother to what is now Arcadia College in nearby Glenside). She maintained a nurturing environment at home, with, as Jim remembers, a sense of order and calm in the house. Both Jim and Carolyn were expected to work hard, do chores (for Jim that included mowing lawns and taking out the trash), and try their hardest to succeed in life.

Both of Jim's parents were supportive and encouraging, particularly relating to school.

* * *

In the late twentieth century, Jim's hometown was known mainly as the United States home of the Swedish, multi-national retailer IKEA. The company opened its first store at the Plymouth Meeting Mall in 1985. Plymouth Meeting was also known by road signs seen by the millions of drivers who each year passed where the Pennsylvania Turnpike (I-276), Interstate 476 (what locals call the "Blue Route"), West Germantown Pike, and Plymouth Road converge. Many ramps, toll booths, exits, and overpasses are located in tiny Plymouth Meeting, which was originally settled in 1686 and in the most recent census was home to a little more than six thousand souls.

The Society of Friends, also known as the Quakers, founded the town, naming it for Plymouth, on the south coast of England, in Devon. The "Meeting" following "Plymouth" refers to the Quaker congregation, services, and building that were founded there. The original name of the village was in fact Plymouth Meeting House, according to local histories.[2]

Jim didn't attend the Plymouth Meeting Friends School in his neighborhood, just down the street. His parents sent him to the public school, Plymouth Consolidated, for kindergarten and then to Ridge Park Elementary, when Jim started first grade. He was only four when he started kindergarten, his birthday being in December. Plymouth Consolidated was a mile from home, and Jim would walk with his mother to school but often made the return trip on his own. From first grade on, he walked or rode his bike each day. These are the quiet signals that Jim grew up in a safe place, in an era simpler than our own.

Years later, at *America* magazine, he would reflect on the historic Quaker building he often passed in his neighborhood:

To a young boy, the meetinghouse was just another building that had always been there. Yet something about it
attracted me. In the cool fall afternoons, I liked to play
with friends in the spacious playground of the school run
by the Quakers. The late afternoon sun, filtered through
the leaves of the immense trees, dappled the cement playground. They had a tire swing there, and you could also
play in the stables and pretend that you were fighting the
British troops.[3]

But as a child he never stepped foot inside.

* * *

Like his parents, he was an avid reader and has vivid memories of anticipating each year's Scholastic Book Fair in his
elementary school. A subscriber to *Jack and Jill* magazine,
he even submitted a poem that was accepted and published
in March 1969 and marks his first instance in print. Jim was
eight.

"Spring"

Spring is fun,
I see the sun;
The flowers grow,
No more snow.
The birds sing—
I feel like a king!

The journey to and from school became a time of introspec-
tion and prayer, even in a boy who wasn't particularly pious.
Jim still remembers, "Nerves about a spelling quiz would
prompt a Hail Mary. . . . If I was worried about a Little

League tryout or a big solo in band practice, I would pray *many* Hail Marys."[4] Other days, he'd walk home with his friend Carol. She was from a Presbyterian family, and Jimmy (that's what she and everyone else, including his family, called him as a boy) would later attend her Christmas Eve services and even participate in her church's active youth group.

As elementary school and junior high school progressed, he was often found at the mall with his friends, playing street hockey, or reading. A favorite author during those years was Jean Shepherd, author of many stories of growing up in Indiana during the Great Depression. His best-known story is "Red Ryder Nails the Cleveland Street Kid," later adapted into the hit movie, *A Christmas Story*. Like Ralphie, the boy in the movie, Jim felt perfectly at home where he lived, in a safe place, among many friends, with parents who cared for him. Still, his family was not the kind that many people would expect would one day produce a Jesuit priest.

"I did not come from a very religious family, at least not the kind that considers themselves 'blessed' if a son decides to become a priest," he later wrote in one of his memoirs.[5]

But he still learned, as a child, to meet God in mystical moments. He tells of the most pivotal of these in *The Jesuit Guide to (Almost) Everything*, as a time when he stopped his bike on a familiar road near home one spring day.

It was a typical meadow in the suburbs, but he suddenly saw it bursting with life: flowers in bloom, grasshoppers jumping. He was alone but realized then that there was so much more. He remembers being ten or eleven at the time. "I felt an overwhelming happiness. I felt so happy to be alive. And I felt a fantastic longing: to both possess and be a part of what was around me. I can still see myself standing in this meadow."[6] Since writing that account, Jim has said, "Sometimes when I pray I return there."[7]

He worked hard in high school, earning excellent grades, doing well on standardized tests, involved in many extracurriculars. By the end of junior year, he was at the top of his class and president of the student government at Plymouth-Whitemarsh High School. In his senior year, he was copy editor of the yearbook and played Hugo Peabody (the part played by Bobby Rydell in the 1963 film) in the school's production of *Bye Bye Birdie*. He was also spending each summer working more than one job to earn the money he would need to attend a good college (mowing lawns, washing dishes, waiting tables, working as a movie theater usher, caddying at a local golf course, and working on a factory assembly line). He applied to and was accepted at the University of Pennsylvania in Philadelphia, just forty minutes from home.

* * *

Jim enrolled, in August 1978, at seventeen, at Penn's Wharton School of Business. He quickly fell in love with Penn: living his freshman year in the Quadrangle, working on the school's humor magazine, and maintaining a large circle of friends, among whom he was quickly known as the witty "lapsed Catholic."

He often frequented the pubs near Penn's campus. Just a month into the start of freshman year he was at one of them, Doc Watson's, getting drunk on the night that Pope John Paul I died in his bed. Jim's roommate, Brad, turning on the radio, told Jim the news after they'd staggered back to their dorm room. "Don't you feel bad you told those jokes!" Brad said, tongue-in-cheek, referring to irreverent jokes he made about Jesus at the bar that evening.

When Jim was ordained several years later, one of his other friends from school asked him, "Do the Jesuits know about those jokes you told at Doc Watson's?!"[8] He would regret the cynicism of those years and the deprecatory way he had approached his faith.

After his first year at his Ivy League university, Jim still had "only a ten-year-old's understanding of Catholicism." And he wasn't curious about other religious traditions. He said, "I was a distinctly uncurious person. It's hard to overestimate how little I thought about real religion." Yet he would, like a typically overconfident young man, argue with an agnostic friend about matters of faith; he remembers that this "served largely to inoculate me against any sort of real relationship with God"—at least, for a time.[9]

The beginning of his sophomore year, the man elected to replace John Paul I, Cardinal Karol Wojtyła, became Pope John Paul II and visited Philadelphia. This was an exciting moment for Jim and his family. "I remember exactly where I was standing: facing the Art Museum, just to the left of the big fountain at Logan Square, over which had been built an immense white altar," he remembers. "I was right next to—really close enough to touch—one of the two colossal Civil War memorial columns on the Ben Franklin Parkway."[10] The day was October 3, 1979, and a million-plus crowd of people was there to see JPII celebrate Mass.

The following day, Jim was interested enough in the Holy Father to rush to Children's Hospital, next to Penn's campus, to see him again.

"It remains one of my most vivid memories of my time in college: Pope John Paul, young and vigorous at 59, in his white cassock, smiling and greeting a row of sick children, many in wheelchairs. I was only about 20 feet away. When he bent down and placed his hands on one young child's head, some of the nurses started to weep. So did I," he later wrote.[11] The desultory Catholic couldn't have been too uninterested in religious matters or too cynical about his church.

He remained a happy college student—studying hard, thinking about his future in the corporate world, smoking marijuana. He also played practical jokes on friends and spent long hours laughing and goofing around both on and off campus. On one occasion, while living in a coed dorm on campus, a friend of Jim's got revenge for a previous practical joke by stealing Jim's clothes while Jim was in the shower and then notifying everyone on the floor to line up and wait for him to have to walk naked back down the long hall to his room, which he did. Studying hard despite his time at Doc Watson's, he was a finance major with an emphasis on accounting.

But then college was suddenly marked by tragedy. Jim writes about it briefly in *In Good Company*. This happened his junior year:

> On Memorial Day, a few weeks after the semester had ended, a good friend and former roommate, Brad, was killed in an automobile accident along with the girlfriend of another friend. Both were twenty years old.

It rocked him. He'd been roommates with Brad Almeda since freshman year, when they shared a room. Sophomore year, it was the two of them plus two other guys; junior year, they all shared a big house off campus with several other friends. In fact, their house on Spruce Street became known for putting on massive themed parties that held hundreds of student guests.

That Memorial Day weekend of 1981, Brad and Michael, another friend from the house, Brad's girlfriend Suzy, and Michael's girlfriend Mindy were all driving in upstate New

York when their car overturned, rolling several times. Brad and Mindy were killed instantly.

"I was just paralyzed with sadness," Jim recalls.[12] Brad, who had just graduated (a year early) and had his whole, promising life ahead of him, was suddenly gone.

In Good Company recounts Jim's feelings a few days later, in Washington, DC, at the funeral:

> During the service, listening to the minister talk about God's love and mercy, I made the decision not to go to church any longer. I decided quickly and clearly. As far as I could see, there could be no rational explanation for a loving God who could do something like this. So why bother with the charade of religion?[13]

That summer was a dark season for Jim. That autumn, returning for his senior year, he had a pivotal conversation with another friend, Jacque Braman, the one person in Jim's group of friends whom everyone regarded as a "fundamentalist." She was, in fact, an evangelical Protestant.

Standing outside the Quad one day after class, Jacque listened carefully to Jim's anger toward God, as Jim still seethed over Brad's death, and responded, "Well, I've been praying to God and thanking him for Brad's life."[14] This was revelatory for Jim. Later that year, he returned to church, with a deeper understanding of what a relationship with God might be about. Jim told me recently:

> After Brad's death, I stayed away from the church for several months, maybe even a year. Jacque's question was a huge challenge to me, and a great grace as well, because until then I saw God as someone who either answered your prayers or rejected them. And Brad's death seemed like the ultimate rejection. I was intensely angry, and perhaps some

of it was a childish anger, as in "Who are you, God, to do this to me?" But most of it was a deep sadness over what I saw as something God had done to all of us. It seemed not only pointless but cruel. Eventually, my Catholic upbringing kicked in and I returned to Mass, mainly because I was afraid God would punish me if I didn't. It took me several more years to come to grips with Brad's death. And it wasn't until I entered the Jesuits that I could see God in a more positive and more personal light—someone who was interested in each of us, not simply an arbitrary cosmic ruler.[15]

* * *

Jim's interests in college also extended to culture and to art. He had always been interested in art, drawing pen-and-ink sketches and painting watercolors from an early age. His artistic interests were further encouraged when he was appointed the art editor for the university's humor magazine, *Punch Bowl*. "James J. Martin" the masthead read.

He was responsible for selecting art for the magazine (a job he'd reprise years later at *America*) and drawing much of it himself. Humor was the aim, in the form of culture criticism, occasional news, and satirical takes on university life. For example, in the April 1982 issue there appeared a full-page reproduction of a faux *New Yorker* magazine cover depicting a lovely and clean Attica State Prison cell complete with corner bathroom sink, hanging spider plant, and bars on one wall. The Attica Prison riot had taken place a decade earlier, in September 1971, and after more than forty people died, New York Governor Nelson Rockefeller initiated necessary changes to the prison system. Media reports had been focusing on the tenth anniversary of the riot just then, in early 1982. That cartoon has a small "J.M." in the bottom right-hand corner.

His humor did not turn often to sarcasm—which is almost de rigueur for university students of any decade and era—except for a few pictorial jabs at the Catholic Church in *Punch Bowl*. For example, he was no great fan of comedian and talk show host David Letterman while in college. "You are never sure if Mr. Letterman's tone is supposed to be 'ironic' or just mocking," he remembered later in the pages of *America*—while praising in contrast a new show hosted by comedian Rosie O'Donnell, whose "fun . . . is at no one's expense."[16]

* * *

Graduating with solid grades at Penn, with a bachelor's degree in economics (BS Econ) with a concentration in finance, Jim was prepared to work for one of the big firms—a large corporation, a financial-center bank or stock brokerage. After interviews in suburban Boston and Winston-Salem, and offers from firms in Chicago, Philadelphia, and Washington, DC, he took a job at General Electric and began work in their highly competitive corporate training program, at the GE building at Fifty-First Street and Lexington Avenue in Midtown Manhattan.

As a boy, he hadn't imagined working for a big company. In fact, he felt he never really understood what his father did, working in "business."

Jim once asked his dad at dinner, "What do you do all day?" and James said, "Well, let's see. I go to meetings, write letters and make phone calls." Jim laughed because it sounded like his dad was doing nothing much at all. But when Jim came home for Thanksgiving one year, soon after starting work at GE, his dad asked, "What do you do at work?" and Jim replied, "Just what you did: go to meetings, write letters and answer phone calls!"[17]

The position at GE was a coveted one for a Wharton grad. Jim's finance and accounting expertise had landed him, first, the internship in the Financial Management Program and then a position in International Finance and Accounting. He would soon move from there to Human Resources with the GE Capital division in Stamford, Connecticut, during a time of tremendous growth for that division of the company. There, he excelled. He was too good a communicator to be stuck in financial management.

One of his supervisors remembers employee Jim as "self-confident without being cocky," "smart—he knew a lot about a lot of things," "quick-witted," and "funny—he was good at smiling and liked to laugh." Also, "he could have a sharp edge. He did not suffer fools gladly, and used his quick mind and sharp wit to impressive effect. His sense of humor could be both cutting and biting."[18]

From New York and later Connecticut, Jim could see his family frequently, taking the train to Philadelphia for all the major holidays and on occasional weekends to catch up with friends. While visiting, he would stay at the family home in Plymouth Meeting. Jim was on the fast track, with an executive position, influence, and authority, living in suburban Connecticut, fulfilling the expectations his parents and friends had for him and that his fine education and hard work had earned him. He was wealthy, young, but also, he found, depressed.

And there were instances, during his time in New York, when he was asked to falsify accounting reports and do other things that made him morally uncomfortable. Eventually, he began to wonder how long he would, or could, do what he was doing for a living. He began to realize that he was no longer happy.

One evening late in 1986, Jim returned home from work late, feeling tired, and turned on the television. A PBS documentary on the life of Trappist monk and spiritual writer Thomas Merton was on: *Merton: A Film Biography*, produced by Paul Wilkes and Audrey L. Glynn.

Jim had never heard of Merton but was quickly rapt, listening to the story of his life. He heard about Merton's autobiography, *The Seven Storey Mountain*, education at Cambridge and Columbia, fathering a child out of wedlock that he then never even saw, living dissolutely, and then seeking life's meaning and ultimately finding that meaning behind the iron gates of a monastery in Kentucky. Jim suddenly had the overwhelming feeling that Merton's way of life was better than his own.

That late evening experience before the television also prompted Jim to see his life as a kind of pilgrimage; his life had importance beyond friendships, earnings, and achievement.

Years later, when he wrote his first memoir describing the events of his entering religious life, he would write that his work was "for anyone interested in finding God in their life and anyone interested in a personal spiritual journey. And that's a journey that everybody ends up taking."[19]

The short documentary had a profound effect on his own life. A few weeks after watching the film and reading Merton's autobiography, Jim began to imagine a religious vocation for himself. Was it possible? Did it make any sense at all? He spoke with his parish priest in Stamford, who suggested he talk with either the vocations director of the Archdiocese of Philadelphia or the Jesuits. Why the Jesuits? The parish priest was a part-time teacher at Fairfield Prep, a Jesuit high school not far from Stamford. A good student, Jim researched the differences. He considered becoming a diocesan priest, because it might be better for his family: he'd still live close by, rooted in a diocese, rather than travel from place to place in Jesuit formation, which, he was learning, could be extensive.

But, then, the Society of Jesus began to exert a stronger appeal, and after he approached the Jesuits on a visit to nearby Fairfield University, he came away with more materials to read. Then, Jim went back to work at General Electric—for two more years.

He once wrote about those intervening years, explaining to his mother in a letter:

> Despite my putting it off and putting it off, the idea kept returning to me. And every time it came back, it was a little bit stronger. I don't know what could be a better example of the Holy Spirit moving you towards a decision. Eventually, I concluded that a life as a religious would be perfect for me, *the* way for me to live my life and do what I felt I needed to accomplish.[20]

Back at GE, he was increasingly disillusioned, looking for something more meaningful, and the stress in his life began to give him stomach pains. His disillusionment led him to seek out a psychologist, with whom he discussed his situation. He recently explained to me:

> In those months, I felt an almost irresistible pull to entering a monastery or doing something more "religious." And I was also growing more dissatisfied with my job day by day. As the stress mounted at work (which brought on a variety of stress-related illnesses) there was this one oasis of calm, which came through reading books by Thomas Merton and C.S. Lewis. So initially it seemed somewhat escapist. Like a place where I could—well, "retreat" is the word that comes to mind. At the same time, I was seeing a psychologist who was helping me understand the reasons

behind my continuing on in a job that I didn't like. So all these forces were working together: a push away from GE, a pull towards religious life and a deepening understanding of some psychological drives (mainly the desire to "go along and get along" and never disappoint anyone). It was one question that a psychiatrist asked, "What would you do if you could do anything you wanted to do?" that unlocked everything for me. It just exploded my whole world.[21]

When he finally contacted the Jesuit vocations director again, in the spring of 1988, he spoke this time in a tone of urgency, asking to be received right away. Suddenly, he felt ready. The vocations director, following protocol, explained how the application process had passed for the coming fall but that Jim could be considered for the following year.

As any good corporate executive would, Jim persisted. He also prayed. A few weeks later, he was grateful to receive another phone call, two weeks after the urgent one, saying he was invited to make a retreat. The retreat, stretching over eight days at Campion Renewal Center, outside of Boston, was another transformative moment: the first time that he had felt a sense that God was inviting him into a "personal relationship," as Jesuits often say.

Following the retreat, the vocations director drove Jim to a Jesuit Ordination Mass at the College of the Holy Cross, in Worcester, Massachusetts, an experience that Jim has said "overwhelmed him."

On August 15, 1988, only a few weeks after completing the long Jesuit application process, he received a phone call telling him that he had been accepted to enter the novitiate. He was learning for the first time how God moves through our desires—an understanding that would deepen in the years to come.

When, in 2018, he talked of "Seven things I wish I'd known at your age" in a commencement address at Loyola University New Orleans, Jim advised the graduates:

> Your deepest desires are God's desires for you. That's how God calls you. Speaking to you through your desires—what moves you, what attracts you, what you're interested in, what gets you up in the morning—is God's way of calling you. So, try not to pay attention to people who say it's all about money or success or impressing people. I've been there and it's a dead end. The better path is one that encourages you to listen to where God is speaking to you.[22]

CHAPTER TWO

Varieties of Spiritual Formation

We are all creatures plagued by unending doubts
and restless, unsatisfied hearts.

—Johannes Baptist Metz

While Jim was trying to navigate his troubles at General
Electric, his father James lost his job at Rorer Pharmaceuticals, an experience that nearly crushed him. James never
quite recovered professionally, and Jim could see his dad's
sadness and disappointment. Then, one sadness followed
another: James and Eleanor separated, with James moving
out of the house.

Jim and his sister were both adults by this time, but the
family turmoil was still painful for all of them. So when all
of Jim's family gathered to support him on "Entrance Day"
into the novitiate, the strain was palpable. Both of his parents and his sister had expressed at various points shock,
surprise, and worry about Jim's decision. This was not surprising. He hadn't discussed his decision with them (or with
anyone) until only a few months before Entrance Day.

Eleanor, Jim's mother, explained to me: "When Jim told me he wanted to be a priest, I was stunned. There was nothing about Jim to indicate that he was thinking about the priesthood."[1] Carolyn, his sister, said: "We really didn't know anyone in the religious life very well. Yes, we knew our local parish priests and nuns, but only well enough to exchange pleasantries (and, in the case of the priests, confess our sins behind a screen!). For us, the idea that Jim would willingly 'give up' having a family (and would also risk a lifetime assignment far from us) was so utterly foreign that we could only assume it would entail a great deal of loneliness on his part. Without a spouse or children, who would love him? Care for him? What if he wound up living in some far-flung mission for the rest of his life and we'd only see him every few years?"[2] It would take the family some time to come to terms with his vocational choice.

Jim entered the novitiate at Arrupe House in Jamaica Plain, Massachusetts, on August 28, 1988. For Jesuits, this is a momentous day. It is one of the three dates inscribed on their tombstones: birth date, entrance date, and the date of death. Jim's two-week "postulancy," a short period of training, in the Society of Jesus began one day later. The novitiate would be considerably longer: two years.

Every Arrupe House is named for Pedro Arrupe, SJ, superior general of the Society of Jesus from 1965 to 1983. Jim knew Arrupe House because he had stayed there once before, the night after he took his psychological tests during the application process. The simple brick building was a former convent. On the second floor was the conference room where novices would gather to learn about St. Ignatius of Loyola, the Jesuit Constitutions, and the Spiritual Exercises. Also upstairs was Jim's first-year room, near the end of the hall, across from the novice director's. Rooms in the former convent were so small that armoires stood outside in the hallway; there wasn't space inside for closets. Rooms on the two floors above were even hotter in the summer; only a few had air conditioning. On the third floor, the airy, high-ceilinged chapel is where Jim first learned to pray. As Jim has made clear in his books, he had much to learn about Christianity, Catholicism, and faith.

Just a few months earlier, in May, he'd said to his therapist that he felt he was making progress in self-understanding. His stomach problems were occasionally intense, and life simply wasn't what he had thought it would be, when he'd planned what he wanted to do after business school. The therapist asked, "What would you do if you could do anything you wanted?" And Jim reflexively said, "I'd be a priest."[3] Now, here he was, in the Jesuit novitiate, having completely overturned his life, hopefully for the better.

Soon, and for the first time, he would learn what it means to enter more deeply into a personal relationship with God. This didn't come through an evangelical "born again" sort of experience. Rather, as a cradle Catholic who had paid little attention to sacrament, story, and services over his first quarter century, it meant discovering for the first time what it felt to be in communion with the living God. As Jim learned to pray in the novitiate, he found that personal relationship. He was also revisiting his love of sketching, which had gone idle since college, often doing some before and after times of prayer.

Jim began to discover how to understand himself in all his own complexities. Once, he revealed to his spiritual director, David Donovan, SJ (simply having a director was another new experience), that he was feeling preoccupied with family matters. His mind and heart were often "elsewhere." There were problems at home in Pennsylvania that weighed on him. He felt guilty about this, thinking that being at Arrupe House, training to become a Jesuit, was a purely spiritual matter. David stopped him and said, "Jim, it's all part of your spiritual life. You can't put part of your life in a box, stick it on a shelf, and pretend it's not there. You have to open that box up and trust that God will help you look at what's inside."[4]

Not all was well. He felt torn, with his parents separated, his father still away from the family home, living now on the west coast. In one poignant letter home to his mother, written at the end of his postulancy, the son explained: "How do I deal with my feelings of abandoning my family [by entering religious life]? It eventually came down to the realization that I couldn't deny what I felt was a strong call, and to do so would just make everyone more miserable. And it wouldn't be fair to *anyone* if I were to put the decision on hold until everything was stable. . . . I would be able to give you *zero* support if I felt as if the family were holding me back. . . . I can give everyone more help if I am strong and happy myself."

There were also some painful phone calls home with his mother, expressing her natural sadness over the family struggles. Another letter from Jim, written three weeks in, explained, "Yes, I will probably have to spend two years close to the novitiate in Boston. But no, they're not my new family."[5]

* * *

Upon arrival in Jamaica Plain, Massachusetts, Jim knew what to expect, at least in terms of dates. He was given this:

Novitiate Schedule
1988–1989

Aug. 28	Entrance Day
Aug. 29–Sept. 9	Postulancy
Sept. 6–9	Postulancy Retreat for First Year Faith Sharing Experience for Second Year
Sept. 12	Regular Order begins
Sept. 26	Apostolic Work and Reflection Group begin
Oct. 7	Province Meeting with Fr. General in the evening at the Immaculate
Oct. 8	Fr. General at novitiate for liturgy, 3 p.m.
Oct. 16	Prayer Days (all at Cohasset)

Further down the schedule appeared:

Feb. 17–May 31   Pilgrimage Experiment for First Year

There were only three novices that year: Jim, Bill Campbell, and another quiet young man who left the novitiate only six weeks in. Jim and Bill didn't get off to an especially good start. Their personalities were different, with gregarious Jim contrasting reserved Bill. They were also several years apart, Bill having only recently graduated from college. Campbell wrote in his journal a week after meeting Jim: "He has a good sense of humor. But he also has the annoying habit of monopolizing a conversation, especially in a crowd, so that it's tough to get a word in edgewise. So tough in a crowd that I've given up trying." But two weeks later, the two men had become good friends—a relationship that has lasted to the present. In Fr. Bill's words today, "I came to hold Jim not just as my Jesuit brother-in-the-Lord, but as my older brother."[6]

Jim was learning quickly and soaking up the life of a member in the Society. Latin phrases describe some of what a new Jesuit first encounters: *primi* and *secundi* for the first- and second-year men, *manualia* for housekeeping, *personalia* for the monthly stipend. During postulancy retreat, when asked to reflect on how and where God had been present throughout his life up until that moment, Jim felt that his eyes and heart were opened wide to powerfully see what he hadn't noticed before. The pilgrimage of his life, since birth, was becoming more and more clear to him.

* * *

On February 15, Jim and Bill, the two remaining *primi*, were sent to Kingston, Jamaica, to assist the Missionaries of Charity sisters who run Our Lady Queen of Peace hospice for sick and dying men and women. He would also teach reading to boys at the Alpha Boys School, a local orphanage run by the Sisters of Mercy. This was to be their "Pilgrimage Experiment for First Year."

Jim was like a fish out of water trying to get wet quickly. His superiors, who all knew his background (suburbs, Ivy League, corporate work in Manhattan and Connecticut), must have thought Jim needed orientation to the grittiness of religious servitude right away. In the fall, they had assigned him to work at a hospital for the seriously ill in Cambridge, Massachusetts, for those same reasons.

It worked. As he later wrote in one of his memoirs about those first weeks in Jamaica, "My job was to clean as many men as I could before their noon meal. I also shaved them and clipped their fingernails and toenails, a job I particularly disliked." Then, he worked cleaning the bathroom. When toilets overflowed, it was Jim's job to scrub the floors clean again. A friend from home visited him once and remarked, "Boy, if your friends from Wharton could see you now."[7]

He continued to face questions from Plymouth Meeting, despite being far away. In one of his first letters home from Kingston, he addressed something his mother had recently asked on the phone: "You had asked me the other night if I have become a 'Jesus freak.'" He concludes, "I feel more comfortable in saying that God is a much bigger part of my life than before."[8]

Jim addressed most of his letters from Kingston jointly to his mother and sister. His dad was still away. One of these begins:

April 30, 1989

Dear Mom & Carolyn,

Actually, I should probably wait until tomorrow to write, so I can date the letter MAY 1, 1989, as in May the month I will return to the States. Do you mind getting the same letter? Oh well, Hard Cheese.

In Jamaica, the noise of the ghetto, especially at night, and the mosquitos, bothered him most of all at first. And the poverty, of a type he had never before seen, unnerved him. The short walk from the Jesuit community of St. George's College, where he stayed, to the middle of the ghetto, where he worked each day, took about ten minutes. "So it shouldn't be too bad—I hope," he wrote his mother.[9]

His work there was remarkably simple. It was both inspiring and devastating; it was servant practice in line with what he was reading so carefully about in the New Testament.

As Jim and Bill's term wound to a close in Jamaica, Jim was more than ready to leave. Grateful for the experience and for what he had learned, yes, but also weary from it. In the same letter home, quoted above, he wrote, "All is well in impoverished Kingston. Only a few more weeks at Mother Teresa's, and I can walk out and never have to clip toenails again."[10]

This sort of honesty has carried through into his books. He speaks openly of emotional struggles during his early Jesuit formation in those early memoirs. Writing honestly and informally and seeking wisdom with an easy familiarity would soon become his trademark style.

* * *

Next in Jim's formation came his first thirty-day guided retreat in the Spiritual Exercises of St. Ignatius, part of every Jesuit's novitiate. This took place at Eastern Point Retreat House, in Gloucester, Massachusetts, in the summer of 1989 and was soon followed by his *secundi* year in the novitiate, which included more prayer, more work with the poor (in the fall at a homeless shelter in Boston), and an extended assignment, called the "Long Experiment," at the Nativity Mission School in New York City, where he worked for several months with high school boys mainly from impoverished neighborhoods on the Lower East Side.

The retreat would mark the beginning of a long association with Eastern Point, a sprawling retreat house complex located on the rocky shores of the Atlantic Ocean in Gloucester, certainly one of the most beautiful settings for prayer in the world. Jim would return here frequently for his annual eight-day retreats (required for Jesuits) for the next few decades and also make his retreat in preparation for both his ordination to the priesthood and his final Jesuit vows at Eastern Point. After his ordination, he would be called on to direct many weekend retreats here, mostly during Lent and Advent. He has called this place, whose natural beauty no doubt appeals to the man who early on found God in nature, his "spiritual home."

In August, at the Church of the Immaculate Conception in Boston, Jim and Bill pronounced their First Vows as Jesuits (poverty, chastity, and obedience), with Jim's family, now more reconciled to his vocation, in attendance.

Next came First Studies. This is when a novice-turned-scholastic (the term for a Jesuit in formation on his way to ordination) undertakes philosophical studies to supplement whatever he previously received in college or university. Jim was sent as a scholastic to Loyola University Chicago for a two-year stint. There, he wrote papers on Plato and Aristotle (ancients), Saints Anselm of Canterbury and Thomas Aquinas (medievals), and Edmund Husserl and Martin Heidegger (moderns). He particularly enjoyed a feminist philosophy class during his second year.

On the home front, Jim's parents had reconciled. In fact, they traveled together on a European trip to cities in Italy and Switzerland, and Jim kept up with them via correspondence, recommending churches and paintings to visit.

One of his teachers at Loyola was Mark Henninger, SJ, who held a doctorate in medieval philosophy from UCLA. Henninger taught Augustine and Anselm. Jim came to know Augustine's *The City of God* and *De Trinitate* (On the Trinity) well. He studied Anselm's *Proslogion* (sometimes titled *Fides Quaerens Intellectum*, or Faith Seeking Understanding) until he could recapitulate the Canterbury saint's famous ontological argument for the existence of God. Jim and Henninger would briefly reunite in Nairobi, Kenya, a few years later when Henninger was on his way to Harare, Zimbabwe, to help start a First Studies school (called a "philosophate") there for English-speaking scholastics.

While in Chicago, as Jim has said: "I spent a good deal of my time . . . hanging out with street gangs." A scholastic was required to work several hours each week in a ministry, outside of philosophy studies. For Jim, the juxtaposition must have been profound. He'd wear an old Jesuit cassock (by the time Jim entered the Jesuits they were no longer wearing these, so he had to hunt one down from one of the older priests at Loyola) into the slums and onto the streets to talk with gang members, guided by members of a Catholic lay organization called Brothers and Sisters of Love.

His mentor in the work was Brother Bill Tomes (Jim writes at length about him in *My Life with the Saints*), the sort of person who, "when gunfights erupted, Bill simply walked in the middle of the shooting until it stopped. . . . Sometimes angry gang members would shout out, 'Brother Bill, get out of the way!' "[11] The wearing of the Jesuit habit was suggested by Bill, who told Jim that merely wearing a black clerical shirt would not suffice. "You'll be more rec-ognizable and they will be less likely to shoot at you." For his part, Bill wore a modified Franciscan habit made from denim patches.[12]

The ministry formed Jim profoundly and was just the balance to studying Aristotle that he required. It put him in mind of Francis of Assisi:

> The more I thought about it, the clearer it became who Bill reminded me of, with his goofy habit and crazy attitude, his penchant for peacemaking, his talk of visions, and his deceptively simple "Love them." He reminded me of Francis of Assisi. I found myself agreeing with [an] older Jesuit. If

Bill is crazy, then he's crazy like St. Francis, and that's a kind of crazy I'd like to be around.[13]

* * *

Jesuit "regency" comes next. This is the stage of formation when a scholastic (or brother) lives and works in a typical Jesuit community for two or three years. Jim was sent to East Africa to work with the Jesuit Refugee Service.

On arrival in Nairobi, assigned to work in the slums, using his business acumen to help the poor create start-up businesses, Jim was excited. But he soon succumbed to homesickness. Always one to make friends easily, he had more to leave behind than most when exiting the familiar for the unknown.

He wrote at that time, "What I was not prepared for was almost total separation from everything that gave my life a sense of meaning and belonging."[14]

This was August 1992, and Jim was at least glad to be addressing his letter to "Dear Mom and Dad and Carolyn and Charles." His parents had reunited, and his sister had married. "Yesterday was a red-letter day, or more specifically a five-letter day," he tells them, "since that is precisely the number of letters I got." Then he speaks of looking forward to settling into the small house he'd soon share with a few other Jesuits. "It is very nice and we already have our beds and desks and kitchen table in. All we have to do is get some living room stuff and we'll be all set. Perhaps I will spend all of my time fixing up the place and working around the yard (we have hibiscus bushes, mango trees, and those immense red flowers you see in wealthy gardens). This would not be a bad way of spending my regency, I think."[15]

This must have been tongue-in-cheek, as he knew there was much trickier work ahead.

Before arriving in Kenya, Jim's education regarding Africa came mostly from CNN, he said. Africans were assumed to be poor, uneducated, Swahili-speaking, likely illiterate, and unkempt. He later admitted he had almost no sense of African cultures, spiritualities, or arts and was blithely unaware of the complexities of real people on the world's largest continent. "American interest in Africa, it would seem, is piqued only during times of crisis," he later explained.[16]

Soon after his arrival, someone handed him a copy of Johannes Baptist Metz's little book, *Poverty of Spirit*, and Jim found that it answered his fears with a kind of spiritual direction. He took, from Metz, the advice not to be afraid of feeling poor in spirit, but to face it head on—something he'd already started to learn while walking alongside Brother Bill in Chicago. "[S]piritual poverty is something to be sought," Jim reflected later, remembering those days. "We seek to develop this honest stance toward life because it leads us to understand how we must rely, ultimately, on God."[17]

He started daily Swahili lessons immediately upon his arrival, taking to it with ease, just as he remembered his French from school well enough to speak exclusively in that language one evening over dinner with two nuns who were visiting from Zaire.

The small house, down the road from the main Jesuit community in Nairobi, was soon fixed up, and they named it Campion House, after St. Edmund Campion, the sixteenth-century English Jesuit martyr. A letter to his parents on September 11, 1992, headed, "Happy Anniversary!"—with continued joy that they were back together—included a carefully drawn illustration of the small complex, with Main

House, Guest House, Papaya Vine, Avocado Tree, and Bougainvillea (thorny vines/bushes with colorful flowers) all neatly labelled. He writes in that letter of still feeling lonely and not having yet found a good friend ("anyone who I could say I confide in") among the other Jesuits. He asks his parents, next time they send a package, to include not the latest *Philadelphia Inquirer* but the *Atlantic* and *New York Review of Books.* "Yes I know I am a snob but I am a missionary so I am allowed a few vices."[18]

Meanwhile, an article written by Jim appeared in the December issue of the *National Jesuit News*—his first piece of published religious writing. It shows topics that would concern him for years to come. For example, he objects to the weak portrayal of St. Ignatius Loyola on a prayer card a friend has received from an aunt in the States: "seated at a desk, quill pen in hand, looking as if the slightest wind might topple him from his seat. *This* is Ignatius?" What would someone who had never heard of Ignatius conclude? "[T]he first Jesuit was a delicate sort, the type of man unused to harsh words or controversies. Not for him the problems of the (gasp) world. . . . I have a feeling a similar fate has befallen most of the saints."[19]

* * *

His work in Nairobi was to help Africans learn to start and run small businesses. The refugees with whom he worked, all of whom had settled in the sprawling slums of the city, had come from all over East Africa. Most other people who work with the Jesuit Refugee Service work on borders, in refugee camps, and therefore minister to populations from a single country. Jim, however, worked with "urban refugees" who had found their way to Nairobi from places like

Somalia, Rwanda, Sudan, Uganda, Ethiopia. It gave him the flavor of not only Kenya but all of East Africa.

He worked in the Income-Generating Projects office, helping refugees manage their varied businesses, often run out of the refugees' small shacks in slums like Kibera, which he visited often. In 1993, seeing the demand for certain refugee handicrafts among wealthy expatriates and visiting priests and sisters, he and a laywoman named Uta Fager cofounded the Mikono Centre (after the Swahili word for "hands"), a small shop that sells goods made by refugees. Decades later, the little store is still running.

One early project was to find designs for liturgical stoles that would appeal to priests working in Africa and then locate refugee-tailors interested in creating them. Jim did the marketing himself. He was a natural entrepreneur and teacher, using skills he'd learned at Wharton and cultivated at General Electric. Other businesses he jump-started, supervised, or coached included a bakery, a women's sewing cooperative, a carpenter's shop, a chicken farm, a woodcarver's shop, and three small restaurants. But most of the business advice he gave was more like Marketing 101, such as, if you're not making enough profits, you either have to increase your price, decrease your expenses, or find new markets. He also used the "Four P's" he learned at Wharton: Product, Price, Promotion, and Place. (Though the Four P's didn't exactly translate into Swahili, as he found out when he led a class with simultaneous translation provided by a refugee.)

Meanwhile, the writing bug had settled in him. Two months after that first article, Jim was writing home to his parents about two other articles, one for *Review for Religious* ("which, I am sure is not on ANY newsstands, so don't bother looking") and his first-ever piece in *America* magazine ("they even put my name on the cover").[20] Also, an article in his alumni magazine, *The Pennsylvania Gazette*, was published at this time: a story of how Jim had graduated Wharton with honors, had gone to GE, became a Jesuit, and now was serving God in Africa. It was the germ of what would become his first memoir. Jim was even sending articles blind to *The Atlantic*, with hopes of becoming an author.

The article in *America*, "The Road to and from Thika," began as a straight question-and-answer interview with a Somali refugee who had made a deep impression on Jim early in his time with the Jesuit Refugee Service. It was, at first, rejected. Thomas Stahel, SJ, executive editor at the time, sent the rejection. "Not understanding how things were done in the magazine world, I simply asked what was wrong with it," Jim recalls. "He replied that a straightforward interview with no context (which I had not provided) would be hard for people to understand, and wasn't particularly compelling. So I rewrote the piece with some context and sent it back. It was rejected again."[21] Meanwhile, Jim had traveled to a small refugee camp in the town of Thika, outside Nairobi, and again rewrote the piece, jumping back and forth from his own experiences in Thika and those of the refugee's. This third try was accepted. It ran in the January 16–23, 1993, issue with the byline, "James Martin, S.J., is working in Nairobi, Kenya, before beginning his theology studies."

The same week the article was published, Jim recorded a cassette tape to send home to his parents. Many people born before 1970 will remember this custom, of chatting onto a tape and sending it to friends or family as a way of replicating being present with them. Jim talked to his parents about life in Kenya and in his religious community, introduced them to his Jesuit friend Jim Corrigan, also working with the Jesuit Refugee Service during his regency, and encouraged his folks to rent the film *Out of Africa* again so that they might be able to picture the lake (Lake Nakuru) he'd recently visited with Jim—"The lake that Robert Redford and Meryl Streep fly over, with all of the pink flamingoes."[22] (Jim would meet Meryl Streep a dozen years later, in 2005, backstage after opening night on *The Last Days of Judas Iscariot*. "It was all I could do not to blurt out, 'I loved *Out of Africa*!' During my time in Kenya, I must have seen it a dozen times on the Jesuit community's ancient VCR."[23])

A second article in *America* ran the next year—a humorous analysis of movies and television programs about priests, ministers, and religious. The major stereotypes were discussed, from "Father Regular Guy" (*M*A*S*H*'s Father Mulcahy) to "Reverend Cranky" (the pastor in *Footloose* who doesn't allow his daughter to dance) to "Sister Saccharine" (the wide-eyed novice in *Sister Act*). This was an article he'd had rejected at *The Atlantic*.

Soon Jim was ill from mononucleosis, thanks to overwork, stress, and perhaps spending time with a refugee or refugees who carried the illness. He spent the next few months of 1993 mostly in bed.

In March, he wrote home to his parents to say, "By the way, I was thinking of expanding 'In Good Company' from the Penn Gazette while I was here. Could you send me a copy?"[24]

They did, and Jim began using the time in bed to write the memoir of his transitioning from corporate life to religious life that became *In Good Company*. The writing was done by early May, and by early June when he wrote to his family in Philadelphia he said he was back at work at the office and shop half days. His parents were concerned about being discussed in the memoir. Jim wrote, midway through that letter: "Oh, by the way, since you're all profoundly worried about my book. Let's say it's a bit premature, since I doubt I will be able to submit it to a publisher for a long time. And don't worry the book is about me, not y'all, so there's little to worry about."[25]

* * *

In East Africa, Jim was homesick, just as he had been in Jamaica. His letters home often showed he was keeping track of how many months were left before he was to return to the States. But there was also tremendous excitement in Africa, including a weekend visit to the Jesuit novitiate in Arusha, Tanzania, to see the First Vows of some East African novices, as well as zebras and giraffes, and a view of Kilimanjaro capped with snow in the remote border country. On weekends Jim would often take the Jeep, either by himself or with his fellow regent Jim Corrigan, and explore the countryside surrounding Nairobi, including visits to the great Rift Valley. And the work with the refugees was fascinating. At that point, he had nine months left to go.

In November 1993, a group of American travelers, including friends of Jim's parents, stopped to visit. Jim was happy to spend time with them and happier still to see them spend their money at the Mikono Centre crafts shop. The shop was doing a booming business, which meant more funds could be plowed back into the refugees' businesses. He sent his visitors home with Christmas presents for his family. Following this, Jim had a rare week of vacation in Mombasa, on the Indian Ocean coast of Kenya, where St. Francis Xavier built a chapel in the sixteenth century during a stay on his way to India. He loved praying in that space. Six months to go.

Then his father, James, suffered a stroke, and when Jim got news of it in Nairobi he immediately requested permission to return home for a visit. His request was denied. Those remaining months would become more difficult.

One morning, Jim opened the crafts shop to discover that the cash box, which was full the night before, was now completely empty. He fell into a rage and quickly blamed his four employees, firing each one, then ransacking their homes looking for the cash. A day later, consumed with guilt and regret, he apologized and rehired three of them. (He always suspected the fourth person of the crime, so didn't rehire him but went on to help him financially for more than a decade.)

Jim would later look back on this experience as a clear example and expression in him of what St. Ignatius calls the "evil spirit." He would also call it, both to his Jesuit friends and later in print, the "worst thing I have ever done."

* * *

In the last months before leaving East Africa, evaluation forms on Jim (called *informatios*) were sent to many of the superiors and colleagues involved, up to that point, in his Jesuit formation. This is a regular part of the process, followed by the provincial (the regional superior) reviewing the reports to see if the candidate is ready for the next stage in formation. For Jim, it would be theology studies. But there were complications.

In the middle of his first year of regency in Kenya, in 1993, Jim had fallen in love. He became confused by his desire to become a Jesuit and his simultaneous romantic attachment. He seriously questioned his vocation, and his provincial then questioned the same in him.

For such a personal matter, Jim has nevertheless discussed it on various occasions. One of these was a mention made while reviewing the 2000 film *Keeping the Faith*, starring Edward Norton as a priest and Ben Stiller as a rabbi, who both fall in love with the same woman. Jim loved the film and said so in the pages of *America*. After mentioning the plot point where the Norton character, Father Brian, confesses his feelings for the woman, Anna, and is then "consumed with both remorse and embarrassment" (Jim's words), Jim reveals:

> All of this put me in mind of something my novice director once told me. The popular understanding of celibacy is not loving, whereas the true celibate loves, and loves a lot. "And if you don't fall in love once in a while, there's probably something wrong with you," he said. The question is what to do with those feelings.[26]

Years later, an interviewer from *The Pennsylvania Gazette*, the magazine of his alma mater, glimpsing Jim's room at America House while on a tour of the building, remarked on the modest twin bed. "Can you get a bigger bed?" the interviewer commented. Jim responded, "Yes, but it would just remind you more of chastity."[27]

More recently, I asked Jim to expand on what happened during that second year. He said:

> It happened when I was in Nairobi, and it happened very quickly. It was also the first (and only) time that I had broken my vows in any sort of serious and ongoing way. But it certainly wasn't planned, and I certainly wasn't looking for it. After a few weeks, it became harder for me, almost impossible, to consider myself a good Jesuit. My conscience in these matters has always been loud and clear. Deafening, really. I remember feeling guilty even walking into the community dining room—like a fraud. There's an implicit trust in religious communities that with the vows—poverty, chastity and obedience—everyone is doing their best.

So when I finally confessed it to my spiritual director, George Drury, it was a great relief. And also a tremendous embarrassment. He asked me a simple question: "What do you want?" He was very gentle. But also very clear: Do you want to leave the Society for this person, or do you want to stay? What kept me in the Jesuits was not that I wanted to reject this person, whom I loved, but that I loved being a Jesuit more. It was probably the hardest decision I've ever made, maybe even harder than entering. It was a sacrifice, too. Let's not underestimate that. But every life involves sacrifices. And every choice is a renunciation of sorts. But in the end, I'm very happy, so it was a good discernment. And the right decision.[28]

But because of the falter, rather than send Jim on to theology, his provincial added another year of regency. Jim felt humiliated. He explained to me:

I was devastated. My approval for theology had already been announced to the rest of the Province. I felt a complete failure. In response, George [Drury, his spiritual director] asked me a question that I've never forgotten and that I've used with young Jesuits since. He said, "How do you view your formation? As a series of hoops to jump through so you can be ordained? Or as a way that God is really forming you?" I had to admit that until then I had seen it in part as a series of hoops. But George helped me to see that this experience, this delay, was, in some mysterious way, part of how God was forming me. In the end, the extra year was spent at *America*, which ended up becoming, after theology studies, my ministry. So without George's question (and without obedience to the Provincial's decision) I wouldn't be in the ministry I'm working in now.[29]

His provincial asked Jim what he thought he might do for that additional year, where he might want to go. It seemed that his time in East Africa, a combination of elation over his ministry with the refugees and confusion about falling in love, was done. And since Jim had become familiar with *America*, and already knew that he wanted very much to write, he suggested the magazine in Manhattan.

"My provincial balked," he remembers, "since it was 'out of province' and also, as I recall, there hadn't been a regent there for many years. Mitigating that was that the superior [of America House Jesuit Community, where both the magazine and its staff were housed] was Father Vincent O'Keefe, who had been Pedro Arrupe's right-hand man. That helped my provincial feel more comfortable about the assignment, and so he missioned me there."[30] The point wasn't so much that Arrupe was still the superior general of the Society of Jesus but that Arrupe was deeply respected, a living saint to many. (In fact, Arrupe's cause for beatification and canonization was officially opened by the Diocese of Rome in July 2018.)

Whereas Jim had first objected to the extra regency year in conversation with his provincial, and even toyed with leaving the Society, he ended up accepting it in the spirit of his vow of obedience, leading him into the ministry he's still engaged in today. He would remember years later that the refugees with whom he worked so closely in Nairobi changed him: how he understands poverty and privilege, how he looks at those who are different from him, how he understands God.

"The refugees broke my heart, too," he said. "[T]hey broke it *open*, helping me to receive God's love in a new way from people I would have never expected to know so well."[31]

* * *

So after two years in Kenya, followed by a brief stopover in Rome to visit his old spiritual director David Donovan, rather than move along in his formation directly to theology studies, Jim went to work at *America* magazine as an associate editor. He moved into America House on West Fifty-Sixth Street, where for decades both the magazine's editorial operations and most of the Jesuits who worked there were located.

It was August 1994. Jim was excited to be back in New York City, a city he'd always loved. In one of his letters home from Nairobi two years earlier, he'd written to his family to say, "I am also homesick b/c I watched *Moonstruck* the other day and thought of our family and also of NYC!" Although he'd lived and worked in Manhattan for years after college, he still felt a "rosy nostalgia for NYC."[32]

America had a venerable history, which Jim already understood. The magazine had celebrated its fiftieth anniversary issue in April 1959, reproducing personal greetings in the form of letters of congratulations from US President Dwight D. Eisenhower; Vice President Richard Nixon; Francis Cardinal Spellman, Archbishop of New York; Jean-Baptiste Janssens, SJ, Superior General of the Society of Jesus; and Pope John XXIII, whose papacy had begun the previous October and who addressed his letter:

To Our Beloved Son
Thurston Davis
Priest of the Society of Jesus.

Thurston N. Davis, SJ, was the editor in chief of *America* in 1959. In 1995, when Jim arrived, George W. Hunt, SJ, held that venerable position. Hunt had written books on both John Cheever and John Updike and so had a reputation as a literary Jesuit, which suited Jim well. He was then thirty-four years old, the youngest editor on staff by three decades. He remembers from that time a conversation at one of the weekly editorial meetings, when editors would review the content of the previous week and topics to be addressed in the upcoming one.

"I noticed something odd," Jim says. "We had run an article about Bruce Springsteen that described him, as I recall, as 'the popular singer and songwriter Bruce Springsteen.' I thought that was really embarrassing. There was no need for such a long ID, as if he were some unknown entity. So I said to the editors, 'This doesn't make sense. We identify Bruce Springsteen as the "popular singer and songwriter Bruce Springsteen." We don't need to say all that.' "

Another editor around the table, clearly Jim's senior, responded, "Well, that's because our readers wouldn't know who he is." So Jim flipped to another article in the same issue and said, "But look at this article, which we just published that mentioned Yves Congar. We don't say 'Yves Congar, the French Dominican and ecclesiologist.' " Another editor replied, "That's because everyone knows who he is," and all the others nodded in agreement. Jim thought to himself, *I'm working in a place where they think everyone knows who Yves Congar is but no one knows who Bruce Springsteen is.*[33]

Almost immediately, George Hunt allowed Jim to build on the article from earlier that year on stereotypes in film and television, with a regular column on media and popular culture. The first column struck a serious tone, noting, "I have recently returned from Kenya," and "I noticed the ambivalent attitude of the West—particularly in the Western media—toward the situation in Rwanda."

But after that, a month later, and recurring weekly, Jim's column was titled, "Television, Etc." Documentarian Ken

Burns's new baseball documentary and *My So-Called Life* on ABC-TV Thursday nights were covered that week. The next two issues saw "Fall Lineup—Part I" and "Fall Lineup—Part II." Jim began to receive advance tapes from publicists of new shows. The tone was consistently and purposefully lowbrow, as in this snippet from a December column that first year, where the virtues of a show are contrasted with the attitude of one of the more prominent Catholic literary intellectuals of the day:

> "The Way of St. James" (Jan. 5) follows the famous 1,000-mile *Camino de Santiago*—the Catholic pilgrimage to the basilica of St. James in Compostela, Spain. . . . We learn about the various legends of St. James. . . . We also run into a woman who stamps *compostelas*, the official "pilgrimage passports." "Say a little prayer to St. James for me!" she calls out in French after novelist David Lodge. Unfortunately, Mr. Lodge seems not to be terribly interested in either prayer or St. James, and his faintly mocking commentary detracts from an otherwise interesting show.[34]

Jim was on a mission to bring youth and cultural understanding to a magazine that its editors knew to have an increasingly aging readership.

As the weekly television column continued, Jim soon also had his first breakout feature: "Opus Dei in the United States." A four-thousand-word article would most likely never appear in the magazine today—it would be rejected as too long—but the 1990s were a time, for *America* as for magazines like *The New Yorker*, when greater space was given to long-feature reporting. At the time *America* also didn't cover breaking news stories, and so there was much more space.

Jim spent four months doing research. When it appeared, the cover of the issue was a solid cherry red. The only type—

other than the name "America" at the very top, with "$1.25"
and "February 25, 1995" in a thin band underneath it—
were two large words in the center in white: "OPUS DEI."
Jim wrote the article because he thought Opus Dei was
little known in the US church and because his fellow Jesuits
at America House, despite being well-educated and informed, knew almost nothing about the Catholic religious
organization when asked about it. "Opus Dei is the most
controversial group in the Catholic Church today. To its
members it is nothing less than The Work of God, the in-
spiration of Blessed Josemaría Escrivá, who advanced the
work of Christ by promoting the sanctity of everyday life.
To its critics it is a powerful, even dangerous, cult-like organization that uses secrecy and manipulation to advance
its agenda." He was writing seven years before Pope John
Paul II canonized Escrivá and eight years before novelist
Dan Brown's *The Da Vinci Code* would reveal the lurid (and
sometimes inaccurate) side of Opus Dei mortification practices to ninety-some million readers around the globe.

Jim interviewed insiders as well as critics. He defined rele-
vant terms such as *numeraries* ("single members who pledge
a 'commitment' of celibacy and normally live in 'centers'
. . . accounting for roughly 20 percent of the membership")
and *supernumeraries* ("married persons who contribute
financially and sometimes serve in corporate works like
schools"). The article included photographs of Opus Dei
institutions, schools, and residencies, including a large house
in tony Newton, Massachusetts, just outside Boston, with
a caption and a pull quote:

Caption: "Brimfield, residence for women numeraries,
Newton, Mass."
Pull quote: "If this is a lay organization, I'd hate to see a
clerical one."

Reader response was predictably strong. Even the startling cover didn't go unremarked in letters to the editor. "The lurid red cover . . . was a pretty good indication of what approach you decided to take toward the organization. After reading the article, my initial impression was confirmed: Opus Dei would not be treated fairly," began one from Rev. Leonard F. Villa of St. Eugene's Rectory in Yonkers. Others were full of praise, including one that covered a page and a half of the magazine from Maria del Carmen Tapia, a former personal secretary to Escrivá, then regional director of the women's branch in Venezuela. Tapia began her missive, "I am astonished that you were able to arrive, through research, at things I learned during my 18 years as a member of Opus Dei."[35]

One week after those letters appeared, there was another by William Schmitt, director of communications, Prelature of Opus Dei, in New Rochelle, New York. Schmitt accused Jim of taking a secular approach to the subject ("the quest for holiness of life is not mentioned once") and of lacking objectivity ("you chose to propagate misconceptions and criticisms").[36] Jim was given column space to respond and did so point by point. The response was headed "Mr. Martin Replies," as he was not yet ordained.

* * *

Throughout that first half of 1995, Jim was probably the hardest working editor on *America*'s staff. His weekly television column continued to appear, in addition to other features and interviews. The needs in Africa remained on his mind in the writing. "You'd have to say the whole continent of Africa is in a chronic state of collapse," reads a large pull quote from a March issue. Two months later, he had another feature, "Who Cares about Africa?," and a few weeks after that, he provided a review of the media's dismal coverage of a growing Ebola crisis: "I spoke to a Zairian friend about the way the media were covering the crisis in his country. 'Most of the time when white people talk about Africa,' he said sadly, 'they speak about "us" and "them."'"[37]

After his two years there, Africa and the refugees would always be topics he was passionate about. But he was also always in touch with current events and popular culture. A March 4 column touched on the salacious murder trial of former football and Hollywood star, O. J. Simpson. Jim began: "As far as Mr. Simpson's trial is concerned, I had hoped I would be able, as some older Jesuits say, 'to pass over it in silence.' However, no one seems able to pass up the opportunity to comment. Least of all me." In one page, his critique of the popular and news media was trenchant. The excuses for covering the trial ad infinitum were reviewed one by one:

> The Customer Is Always Right Excuse.
> [W]e cover the trial because people want to see it. . . .
>
> The Dog-Eat-Dog Excuse.
> We cover the trial because we have to; our competitors are covering it. . . .
>
> The Rumpole of the Bailey Excuse.
> We cover the trial because it is a way for people to learn more about . . .
>
> The Margaret Mead Excuse.
> We cover the trial because it is a great expositor of the social ills facing our complex, contemporary world: racism, crime, greed, etc. *O tempora! O mores!* . . .

Always, there was humor and wit—biting, in this case.

"Jim was a talented self-starter," said Thomas J. Reese, SJ, who later replaced Hunt, becoming editor in chief and Jim's boss, "so he did not need a lot of direction. He would frequently come and talk to me about a proposed project, which I would always support. Honestly, sometimes I wasn't sure the project was a good idea, but I had enough trust in Jim that I gave him free rein and he never disappointed me."[38] Jim's critique of the Simpson trial coverage concludes: "Oh, and speaking of the problems of our complex, contemporary world: Remember Bosnia? How about Rwanda? Sorry, they've been pre-empted by the trial. Tune in next year when we will rejoin our regularly scheduled world, already in progress."[39]

* * *

The following fall, now approved by his provincial to continue his formation, he moved to Cambridge, Massachusetts, for his theology studies at Weston Jesuit School of Theology, just off Harvard Square. He lived in the Jesuit community in the 2200 block of Massachusetts Avenue but continued to write for *America*. His reputation as a culture commentator was already in place. In one jaunty piece on how it's sometimes good to relax in front of the television, he discussed Martha Stewart, Captain Kangaroo, and Julia Child: "Word has it that Julia Child lives near me in Cambridge, Massachusetts. I have a recurring fantasy of bumping into her at the supermarket, professing my admiration, and having her say, 'Well, that's so kind of you. Will you let me prepare a meal for your Jesuit Community?' (And on *my* night to cook!)" When this piece was licensed and excerpted to run in *Catholic Digest*, the largest circulating Catholic magazine in the country, however, the contents page didn't even note Jim's name. The days of fame as a writer were still to come. It simply read: "'TV as Tranquilizer' Stressed Out? Try the Tube—*America*."[40]

Also from Cambridge, Jim wrote about purchasing and wearing a clerical collar: "Collared" could easily have appeared in a humor magazine. Lamenting the decrease in the number of Catholic seminarians in the United States, Jim refers to an ad campaign in one archdiocese featuring the fictional Father Guido Sarducci of *Saturday Night Live* to make the priesthood seem cool again. He also tells of a sales clerk disbelieving him when he says he's in seminary and needs collared shirts for reasons other than costuming. And he describes being propositioned by a woman at a party:

> (Did I look good in black or was I just a more challenging quarry?) After a polite rebuff she asked, "if it wasn't too personal," was I an alcoholic? And, "if it wasn't too personal," was I gay?

"Most of the time people seem to be simply mystified," he goes on to say.[41] The article is still laugh-out-loud funny all these years later. His take on culture was frequently mixed with a rare gift for humor and irony without sarcasm.

Jim often referenced his theology studies and professors. In a review of a new show, *The Holy Grail* on the Learning Channel, he wrote of watching with his distinguished professor of church history, John W. O'Malley, SJ: "I thought it might be instructive to watch with him to see what he thought of its history. Not much, as it turned out." Then, he quotes the professor's reaction of the show: "It's a travesty, in that it presents good guys and bad guys: the utterly evil Catholic Church and these innocent bystanders. But television does that all the time."[42]

At other times, there wasn't so much humor as cleverness, and then the gift in the writing is an absence of anger. "The Rich Are Different" surveyed how the lives of the rich and famous are glorified in the pages of magazines and on television in increasingly distorting ways. "Is it just me, or have the 80's returned?" he began. In the pages of *Newsweek*, *The New Yorker*, and *Vanity Fair*, and in sixty-second commercials for diamonds, credit cards, automobiles, and gourmet pet food, he found an "abject devotion to affluence" and distortions of where to find happiness. He writes like a soon-to-be priest: "The rich are our new saints. The poor are, at best, disqualified from life." But he also writes as a critic of politics and culture. It was January 1996: "I can't help wondering if this has anything to do with the Zeitgeist blowing through Washington. Now, with Newt Gingrich ascendant, the rich can feel comfortable about being superior to the poor and keeping apart from them. . . . 'In life there are drivers and passengers,' says the Volkswagen television ad. 'Drivers wanted.' Passengers need not apply."[43]

That priestly voice continued intermittently. One September 1996 television column has Jim criticizing the new network MSNBC for running on the screen references to the new worldwide web. "[R]epeated references to something that only the affluent are able to afford can come off as elitist. The information highway, for all the hype and hyperbole, doesn't make stops in poor people's homes."[44] A few years later, at the end of the first season of the first popular reality TV show, *Survivor*, he devoted a column to the trend, concluding, "Where will this end?" He predicted that sex, executions, and murders would soon be seen in real time on television: "And all of this will be explained away by networks that tout the value of 'reality.' . . . How sad. Because overall, we could probably survive with a little less reality and a little more morality."[45]

* * *

In addition to all of this writing, he worked hard and successfully as a student at Weston. His parents (and Wharton) had instilled in him strong study habits. A friend remembers, "During our third year we were in a study group with a few other students to prepare for comprehensive exams. I jokingly say that I taught Jim everything he knows, but the truth is that Jim was in the group to befriend and support us! It was clear that oral communication was an area of excellence for him."[46]

As part of his formation, he was still asked by his superiors to participate in "outside ministries" in addition to his studies. While in First Studies at Loyola Chicago, those ministries would be, during the first year, working with street gang members and the second year with homeless men and women in a local community center. During theology studies Jim would spend several hours a week at the Suffolk County House of Corrections, a jail in downtown Boston. Working with his friend George Williams, who had entered the Jesuit novitiate one year ahead of him and who was working full time at the jail, Jim led weekly Bible study sessions for both men and women inmates, counseled them individually (not being able to hear confessions since he was not yet ordained), and visited men in the "hole," solitary confinement, to encourage them and speak to them about their faith. Weston marked a fruitful time for him both intellectually and spiritually.

But midway through his theology studies, Jim began suffering increasing migraines and was worried enough to see a doctor. He was also, by his own admission, a bit of a hypochondriac then. But, indeed, an initial scan showed evidence for concern—enough so that further procedures were ordered. A small tumor under his jaw was to be removed, and Jim took the advice of a Jesuit physician friend and traveled to Chicago to have the procedure done in his friend's hospital. In Chicago, he explains, "Fear welled up within me, and with it self-pity." With that fear, lying on the surgery table, came an intense desire: "I hope I don't die, because I want to be a priest!"[47]

When he woke up and then recovered easily, he took from the experience something that would mold him intensely, informing his teaching and writing as well as his spiritual direction years later: "Naming our desires tells us something about who we are. . . . Expressing these desires brings us into a closer relationship with God. . . . When we tell God our desires, our relationship with God deepens."[48]

* * *

There must have been a measure of ambition driving Jim to do so much and then to think about writing a book as well. No author writes simply from a charitable desire to communicate, even an author who is living by vows. There's always at least a bit of ego involved.

His first book began in the pages of *America*. Soon after starting at Weston in Cambridge, his article "How Can I Find God?" was published in the magazine; it includes the answers of well-known and respected Catholics, Protestants, Jews, laypeople, clergy, Jesuits, theologians, spirituality writers, and psychiatrists: historian Martin E. Marty, Harvard professor Robert Coles, fiction writers Andre Dubus and Jon Hassler, Holocaust survivor Elie Wiesel, theologians Pheme Perkins and Catherine Mowry LaCugna, and others.[49]

Then, seventeen months after the first "How Can I Find God?" article, there appeared another special installment in *America* announcing that a book was forthcoming from

Triumph Books/Liguori Publications and providing the answer of, among others, Cardinal Joseph Bernardin to the title question. "[He] wrote his essay in the summer of 1996," the introduction to the installment read, "a few months before it was discovered that his cancer had recurred. It is published here for the first time."[50]

Patricia A. Kossmann, an editor at Triumph/Liguori, had taken notice of Jim's work at *America* and wrote a letter he was thrilled to receive. She was offering to publish a book. *How Can I Find God? The Famous and the Not-So-Famous Consider the Quintessential Question* appeared in May 1997. Years later, Kossmann came to be the literary editor at *America*. Jim had kept in touch with her and knew that she was looking for a new position. "I told Tom Reese about her, and said what a great editor and wonderful person she was, and we brought her on as our first full-time woman editor," he remembers.[51]

There would be one more installment of "How Can I Find God?": a cover story drawing from the upcoming book, featuring novelists Frederick Buechner and Ron Hansen, Catholic sister and activist Helen Prejean, and one of Jim's beloved professors from Weston, Daniel J. Harrington, SJ. This time, the introduction and responses from the notable included a toll-free number for calling the publisher to buy a copy of the book.[52] Ads at that time also pictured the editor, Jim, with a nearly full head of brown hair.

* * *

The summer after his first year of theology studies saw him back at *America* in New York, interviewing Croatian Catholic Franjo Komarica, bishop of Banja Luka. The bishop was in the United States to testify before a congressional commission and meet with congressional leaders to ask for financial assistance for his people. The Croat-Bosniak War took place between October 1992 and February 1994. As Jim reported in the introduction to his interview in August 1996, "[Bishop Komarica] remained in his diocese throughout the war, during the 'ethnic cleansing' that took place in the region."

Then the humor without sarcasm began to change. As theology studies were winding down and ordination to the priesthood was nearing, Jim's take on culture became increasingly judgmental, not unlike the way a young Thomas Merton in his early writings often looked askance at the world he'd left behind. Jim was finding greed and dishonesty everywhere—and warning his growing audience of readers to avoid the same. There was the television column in which he took to task Apple computer's new advertising slogan, "Think different," and how those two words were paired with images of famous creatives and remarkable people, such as Albert Einstein and Mohandas Gandhi: "One wonders . . . whether the famously ascetic Gandhi would have seen the need for an Apple Powerbook 3400c/200,16/2GB/CD, currently priced at $3,599.99." And, after mentioning Rosa Parks in one of these ads, Jim wrote: "It's good to know that Rosa Parks's courageous gesture of defiance is helping Apple sell more computers." Then, the soon-to-be priest preaches:

> But "different" implies that you don't run with the pack. And not running with the pack would mean that you would refrain from making decisions based on a television commercial. In other words, people like Pablo Picasso and Thomas Edison got where they were through independent thought, not by buying something that they saw on television.[53]

Sixteen months later, he would write of no longer owning a computer and not having email, because the tendinitis in his hands had made typing too painful, but he also reminded readers of the benefits of slowing down. That column began, "Bless me, Bill Gates, for I have sinned."[54]

Sometimes his disdain for consumer values was combined with an enthusiasm for popular culture, which confused some readers who easily link the two. For instance, he praised the satirical animated sitcom *The Simpsons*, which most people his age and older found offensive, saying that "their writers are surprisingly astute social critics."[55] And he continued to review positively shows, plays, and performances that struck more traditional Catholics (or, simply, older ones) as distasteful. He was on the lookout for ways that Christian values or the Gospel story were on display, despite a cultural milieu that may seem foreign or offensive.

A Manhattan Theatre Company off-Broadway production, *Corpus Christi*, now a mostly forgotten play, received a vigorous defense in *America* from Jim. "Twelve actors portray gay men, who themselves portray characters taken from the Gospels," he explained, and organizations such as the Catholic League for Religious and Civil Rights should be willing to see a work of art (which they hadn't) before bothering to publicly condemn it (which they had), he argued.[56] He added: "Protest rallies are held almost daily at the theater, complete with gray-robed friars leading recitations of the rosary"—a veiled reference to the Community of the Franciscan Friars of the Renewal (CFR), founded in the Archdiocese of New York by, among others, popular priest, author, and media personality Rev. Benedict Groeschel. The Catholic League's president, William Donohue, protested in a letter to the editors one week later. In contrast to Jesuits, Donohue essentially said, the priests of the

CFR "are among the most dedicated" and "deserving of our emulation."[57]

So, the soon-to-be-priest was playing a part in the culture wars.

* * *

When he completed his theology studies in 1998, Jim was ordained a deacon and then returned to New York. He split his time between *America* as an associate editor and at the Church of St. Ignatius Loyola for his "pastoral year" before ordination to the priesthood. Jim loved serving at St. Ignatius, and still does to this day, particularly because it is a large, active parish with a team of talented pastoral ministers. And he loves to preach, which he did often that year, concentrating on shorter, well-prepared homilies.

The experience wasn't without uneasiness, however. In one of his many "Of Many Things" *America* columns that year, he recounted a conversation he had with a "self-proclaimed liberal" who had heard him preach the previous week. She accused him of clericalism: enjoying the high pulpit, relishing the role of instructing others on what to do or how to think.[58] Mistrust and combativeness seemed to be spreading in the church.

A deacon wears a Roman collar, which suited Jim fine. Throughout regency, he'd commonly worn khakis and cardigan sweaters. The snappy-dressed Fr. Martin that would become common in the media a decade later was still a long way off. (By the way, Jim has written: "When I am photographed not in clerical attire, it typically prompts angry letters and phone calls to the offices of our magazine asking if I'm ashamed to be a priest."[59]) Always honest and self-deprecating, during the transitional diaconate year he reflected humorously in another "Of Many Things" column (he was occupying this first page in the magazine frequently since Tom Reese had become editor in chief):

> I was running to catch the bus, late for an appointment at the parish. As I approached . . . I saw, to my dismay, the bus pulling away. I dashed across the busy street and caught [it] at a stoplight. Positioning myself at the door, I knocked insistently to attract the driver's attention. He turned to scowl at me and shook his head disdainfully, refusing to open the door, though he had stopped at a light. Not wanting to be late for our weekly parish staff meeting, I slowly unzipped the top of my windbreaker, revealing my new R.J. Toomey tab-collar, 65/35, black, short-sleeved clerical shirt, and put on what I call my Gerard Manley Hopkins face: wan, overworked and altogether meek. Miraculously, the bus doors parted.[60]

Among his other duties as a deacon, Jim began leading a monthly book club for young adults at St. Ignatius Loyola. With young New York City professionals, he'd gather to eat pizza and then discuss Kathleen Norris's *The Cloister Walk*, Ron Hansen's *Mariette in Ecstasy*, Cardinal Bernardin's *The Gift of Peace*, Dorothy Day's *The Long Loneliness*, and Patricia Hampl's *Virgin Time*. The book club would expand into groups for both young adults and adults, continuing for ten years at the parish, with Jim leading parishioners to read dozens of books on the Catholic faith.

It was no accident that many of the books were spiritual memoirs, as Jim usually selected them and this was one of his favorite categories. He'd also learned to write memoir in ways that are disarming for a priest, and that would lead to the popular reception of whatever he had to say. Memoir became Jim's most adept and common way of expressing his most important insights. As one example, consider this paragraph written on the subject of what he learned after his first year of priestly ministry:

> The second lesson [I learned] had to do with hearing confessions. . . . I can report that a certain newly ordained priest spent far too much of his time in the confessional yakking away at his penitents. Yak, yak, yak. By chance, he stumbled upon a fine new book called *A Confessor's Handbook*, by Kurt Stasiak, O.S.B., and under "Some Things to Avoid" read this line: "Do not say too much." And like St. Augustine picking up his Bible in the garden, the newly ordained priest knew instantly that these sublime words were directed toward him. So lesson two: listen.[61]

The anecdote is told entirely for the purpose of that last, short line.

* * *

There is a good reason why this chapter is the longest by far in this book: it takes a long time to become a Jesuit priest.

Saturday, June 12, 1999, saw Jim become Father Martin at the Church of St. Ignatius at 28 Commonwealth Avenue, Chestnut Hill, Massachusetts. The parish is a part of Boston College (across the street) and is run by the New England Jesuits on behalf of the Archdiocese of Boston. The Most Rev. Lawrence Burke, SJ, a Jesuit of the New England Province, presided at the ordination of six Jesuits that day. Burke was Jamaican-born, and, as a New England Province Jesuit, was then a natural for the Province's missions, which were in Jamaica, Iraq, and Jordan. The same month as Jim's ordination, Bishop Burke was named the Archbishop of the Archdiocese of Nassau, the Bahamas, where he had already served. Writing about that day a few months later, Jim told this story about Burke:

> [A]t the very close of the liturgy, in a moving gesture, the bishop knelt down and asked for the blessings of the newly ordained. Then he did something else.
>
> "What's going on? What's going on?" asked George [an agnostic friend of Martin's in attendance], craning his neck to see the proceedings.
>
> "The bishop is kissing Jim's hands," said Bruce [a Catholic, Jesuit-educated friend, sitting beside George] helpfully. "And get a good look, because it's the last time *that's* going to happen!"[62]

Jim's parents were there, and his younger sister Carolyn, her husband Charles, and their infant son, Charles Joseph. Eight days later, Jim celebrated his First Mass back at St. Ignatius Church in New York City. By now his family fully supported his Jesuit vocation and happily participated in the Ordination Mass, with his sister serving as lector, or reader, during the Mass.

His two nephews, Charles and then Matthew, born seven years after his older brother, would figure prominently in Jim's writing and, more important, his life. If he was close to his parents and his sister, he felt as much affection for his young nephews and wrote years later how they "profoundly deepened his appreciation for the mystery of life."[63]

Eleven months after his ordination, the Jesuit vocations office in Washington, DC, took out an ad in *America* with a large photograph of Jim and two friends (Karen Smith and Paula Fitzgerald, classmates from Weston) from the ordination Mass, all smiles, the caption reading, "James Martin, S.J., celebrates his first Mass," and a headline, "Come and share the Jesuit vision."[64]

CHAPTER THREE

Journalism and Vocation

With priestly ordination came an assignment to work for *America* permanently, and Jim's experience and reputation at the magazine grew. Over the course of his first twenty years in journalism, his masthead titles there moved chronologically through associate editor, culture editor, acting publisher, associate editor, and then editor at large. From then until the time of this writing, he has never taken a leave of absence.

The decade of the nineties showed a burgeoning interest in spirituality and the reflection of the same in a proliferation of television programs, films, plays, books, magazines, and other media. One of Jim's colleagues at the time, Phyllis Tickle, who founded the first department of religion at *Publishers Weekly*, the bookselling and publishing industries' trade journal, took to calling books "portable pastors." That was one way to describe both the reason for and effect of the popularity of spirituality, and how it began to track with declines in participation in organized religion.

Jim was tracking these trends as well as anyone—most often through his weekly television reviews column. One round-up from the summer of 2000 described what he called the "most surprising new trend" in television: movies about Jesus on the major networks. CBS, NBC, and ABC all broadcast one the year before: CBS's was a miniseries, and ABC's was a clay-animation film. With characteristic humor, he summarized:

> At times it was difficult to keep up with all the Christological activity in the television industry. But I can happily report it made for highly entertaining conversations with network representatives. At one point, after chatting with an ABC publicist about their upcoming Claymation special, I mentioned that I had already watched the CBS movie, "Jesus."
>
> "Oh please!" she sniffed, "*Jacqueline Bisset* as Mary?" In response, I suggested that this casting decision was probably not something to mock, given that *their* Mary was, in point of fact, a five-inch clay doll.[1]

After his ordination, the journalistic work seemed unchanged. The subjects that interested him had been formed years earlier. Africa remained ever-present. A cover story in early January the following year demonstrated this: "The Hidden Holocaust: An Interview with Sudanese Bishop Macram Max Gassis." This quote from Bishop Gassis appeared in large print on the cover of the magazine:

> We are called a "recipient church," and we are. And the church in the United States says it is a "donor church." And it is. But aren't we also a donor church? What about our blood—the blood of our martyrs? What about the suffering of our children?[2]

Jim had learned to write before joining *America*'s editorial staff, but he learned to be a journalist by tutelage with seasoned journalists there—most of all, George W. Hunt, SJ (1984–1998), his first editor in chief, and Thomas J. Reese, SJ (1998–2005), his second. There was great respect for Jim's creativity, energy, and talent among the editors. One senior editor, John Donohue, SJ (whom Jim described as a saint in an obituary after Donohue died in early 2010), used to playfully call his younger colleague "Mister Martin" during his first year at the magazine, when Jim was still in his regency. But a few days after he was ordained, Donohue, seeing him for the first time, greeted him, "Good morning, Father!"

* * *

Jim's cover article in March 2000, "Anti-Catholicism in the United States: The Last Acceptable Prejudice?," is an example of his gifts for religion journalism. Reflecting thorough research and marshalled opinion, he identified examples in the culture where anti-Catholicism was evident, offered historical understanding of how the prejudice originated and became acceptable, and summarized where the prejudice rests in mistaken assumptions. For example:

> First, in any democracy there is a natural distrust of organizations run along hierarchical lines, as the Catholic Church surely is. The church's model of governance can strike many as almost "anti-American." . . . Second, the church's emphasis on community . . . is often seen as at odds with the American ideal of rugged individualism. This attitude manifests itself whenever the institutional church is criticized but personal faith is celebrated.[3]

He would repeat the effort a month later, filling two full pages of the "Forum" section of the *Pittsburgh Post-Gazette* with the same article. Even William Donohue, the president of the Catholic League who had sparred with the younger Martin over a film his organization had protested, wrote a letter to the editors of *America* to say, "Father Martin's contribution is one of the best to appear in a long time."[4]

Jim's relationships with friends and family continued, as ever. Then his father died. James Martin Sr. succumbed to cancer on July 28, 2001. It was a slow and painful passing. As he approached death, lying in a care facility, he became more attentive to religious matters. He asked for prayers and talked about heaven. "My dad also became more gentle, more forgiving, and more emotional," Jim has said.

It was both a healing time for father and son and a charged time for Jim. He found the changes in his father consoling but also confusing, coming late in their relationship. Jim observed, however, that "vulnerability is another way in which we can experience our desire for God."[5] His father's funeral, celebrated at his family's home parish of Epiphany of Our Lord, in Plymouth Meeting, would be his first funeral Mass, coming not long after his ordination.

* * *

On September 11, 2001, when terrorists hijacked airplanes and flew them into the World Trade Center in New York City, at the Pentagon in Washington, DC, and in a field southeast of Pittsburgh, the world came to a stop. Jim was in New York City that day at America House, where he lived and worked, about six miles north on Manhattan Island from the World Trade Center.

He reflected two months later in the *New York Observer* on what he'd done the day before. September 10 he was pondering asking an editor at the *Wall Street Journal* if they'd decided to run the humorous article he'd submitted "skewering Jack Welch, the former chief executive of General Electric and a newly minted author. The media, I suggested, were portraying the life of Mr. Welch in the same way that hagiographers of old treated the lives of the saints and had, in effect, canonized him while still on earth."[6]

But the morning of September 11, sitting in his office, Jim spent most of the day stunned by the news and live coverage. He had a doctor's appointment scheduled for ten o'clock in the morning, which he kept, not knowing yet the extent of what was happening. Otherwise, he was glued to the television until dinnertime when the house's usual cook didn't show up. So Jim cooked a spaghetti dinner for his community.

By nine o'clock that night, still without any instructions from the Jesuits or the archdiocese as to what priests should do to respond, he made his way, in his collar, to St. Luke's-Roosevelt Hospital Center. Expecting to help in some way by ministering to the injured, he didn't find any. He then walked to the Javits Center, where it was said some injured had been taken. The streets were nearly empty until he reached the Javits where there were suddenly swarms of police officers and rescue workers. Again, he found he wasn't needed, but a bus driver told him that Chelsea Piers was where survivors had been taken. So Jim boarded a bus, all alone, and was driven downtown to a triage center.

At Chelsea Piers, now in the company of other priests and friars who had had the same thought to help, he discovered there simply were not many survivors after all. Around midnight, a police officer approached and said, "I don't think there will be anyone coming, Father."[7] So Jim walked all the way home.

The following day, September 12, he worked at St. Vincent's, a family counseling center in the city. His boss, Tom

Reese, looking back on that time, says: "Jim immediately asked me if he could go down and minister to the injured. I, of course, said yes. He went down to a hospital where he waited with the staff for the injured. No one came. They were all dead. The following day he began ministering to the first responders. I was very proud of Jim. He is not just a great writer, he is a great priest."[8]

On September 13, Martin returned to Chelsea Piers where he quickly discovered—and was told—there were already plenty of clergy. Then, a police officer offered him a ride in his squad car to what we now know as Ground Zero.

Winding through the streets of Lower Manhattan, the streets became dustier and Jim began to see signs of the devastation. Smoke was still pouring out of the space where the Twin Towers had recently stood. "Then suddenly he makes this turn, and there we are in the middle of hundreds of firefighters and rescue workers and police officers. I remember thinking that I had never seen so many uniforms in my entire life. Army people and just everything, everything you could imagine, every uniform you could imagine. Just this sense of chaos and panic and danger, as well," Jim told an interviewer from Columbia University a month later.[9]

Jim would realize later that grieving his father's death had helped prepare him for what he witnessed at the site of the 9/11 tragedy. Not only the sadness and the grief, but the way that his father reconciled with his faith at the end. "I came to Ground Zero with an understanding of the miraculous way that grace works," Jim said. "A lot of people are more open to it when they're in difficult situations, when their egos are stripped down. I really believe that."[10]

He was taken to a morgue that had been set up for the thousands of bodies being recovered and processed. Jim took one look inside and realized, "I couldn't possibly work in the morgue. But what I *could* do is minister to the rescue workers."[11] He spent September 13 talking with, ministering to, the police officers, firefighters, and rescue workers in and around the Ground Zero morgue.

On October 1, the news section of *America* displayed headlines, "Nation Moves from Terror to Prayer," "Muslim Theologians Say Attacks Cannot Be Justified Under Islam," and "K. of C. Gives $1 Million for Families of Rescue Workers." The cover story, "The Laying Down of Life," Jim wrote based on what he had seen and who he'd spoken with on that first sunny day, September 13, at Ground Zero.[12] Describing what he saw in an eerie first-person voice, he writes:

> Leaving is stranger than coming. All I have to do is walk north. The rubble eventually recedes, so there is nothing to step over; the soot becomes less distinct and the pavements are cleaner; the smoke clears and I remove my mask; there are more and more pedestrians. And then I am back in New York on a sunny fall day: people in Greenwich Village sit in outdoor cafes; women in tank tops jog by; taxis race past. I remember reading about soldiers in World War I who would fight in the trenches in France during the day and then, granted a day's leave, would be in the theaters of London in the evening.[13]

* * *

The following year saw the breakthrough for the Jesuit journalist, when he began to reach an audience well beyond that of a typical Catholic spiritual writer. What was it about James Martin, SJ, that led to relative stardom?

It is possible to identify a few factors. He was well-placed, living in New York City. He was well-spoken and had been since high school. He was smart, bright, confident, warm, and friendly, all qualities that translated well to producers and editors seeking expert opinions from people with TV-friendly faces. And he had friends in every corner where influence matters in the media, given his role at a weekly magazine, albeit a religious one, in New York City.

In March 2002, Jim made his first appearance on *CNN Saturday Edition*. It was Easter Eve, and he was there to discuss the role of organized religion in the post-9/11 world. The still-young priest appeared on screen beside the aging Protestant evangelist and Moral Majority founder Rev. Jerry Falwell and the venerable Rev. James Forbes, senior minister of historic Riverside Church in New York City.

When host Andrea Koppel began by asking Falwell if Christians were supposed to "turn the other cheek" in response to the terrorist attacks, and if a similar response might work in the increasingly turbulent situation between Israelis and Palestinians, Falwell replied that all Christians should be praying for peace in Jerusalem. Then he added, "And I think that unless something happens very radically and very quickly, Israel and most of that part of the Middle East is in for a bloodbath."

Next, Koppel turned to Jim. She asked: "How could a loving God let so many innocent people die as they did September 11?" This was clearly a segment meant to provoke feelings and spark quotable comments from experts. Jim was half the age of Falwell and Forbes, but his response showed an uncommon maturity:

> Well, that's a very difficult question. That's the question of evil in the world. And I think the more important question is, what is the believer's response to a situation like September 11?
>
> I worked down at Ground Zero for a few weeks afterwards, and what I saw was not only the presence of evil,

as evidenced by the destruction of the World Trade Center, but also the presence of good and the presence of God's grace, which brought together so many people in works of charity.[14]

Significant invitations continued to come in. In July 2002, Jim appeared in *The New Yorker* on "The Mail" page, responding to an article that had appeared in that publication about lapsed Catholics. This must have been a thrill for someone who grew up admiring the magazine of Harold Ross, William Shawn, and Katherine White.

And that September, at the one-year anniversary of 9/11, a review of Jim's third book, *Searching for God at Ground Zero*, just published, ran in *USA Today*. Reviewer Bob Minzesheimer wrote: "It's a welcome antidote to the instant histories and souvenir-like illustrated remembrances stacked on the 9/11 tables at bookstores. *Searching for God* is less about the evil of the attack than the charity, hope and grace among the community of rescue and recovery workers and volunteers."[15]

Searching for God was a journal of day-by-day experiences at the site. Without easy answers, Jim wrote that both those who doubt God's presence in the world and those who doubt the presence of evil should come to where the World Trade Center once stood.

Also that month, a full-column profile of Jim appeared in the *New York Observer*, written by his friend Terry Golway. It mentioned two books: *In Good Company* ("chronicling his transition from Manhattan yuppie to Jesuit priest") and *Searching for God* ("in essence, a journal of Jim's ministry to [and from] the heroes of 9/11"). Fr. Jim had become an expert in religious matters, including the Roman Catholic Church, but he was also seen as a priest of importance to everyday people, beyond the church, and an intriguing public personality. Even a sketch of "Jim Martin" in Roman collar, broadly smiling, accompanied the article.[16]

* * *

Books two and three appeared in rapid succession. The second book was a memoir, telling the story of why he left the corporate world of General Electric to become a priest and member of the Society of Jesus.

The title, *In Good Company*, is a clever play on a phrase St. Ignatius used to describe the Jesuits, *Compañia de Jesús*, the Company of Jesus—reminding one of a military company, reflecting the founder's soldiering background. The "in-house" magazine of the American Jesuits was until recently called *Company* magazine, where many James Martin articles appeared over the years. (It ceased publication in 2010.) Then-editor of *Company*, Ned Mattimoe, SJ, suggested that his friend, Jim, then a philosophy student at Loyola University Chicago, write an article for *The Pennsylvania Gazette* with that title. The *Gazette* ended up using a different one for its article, but the title stuck for the book.

As mentioned in the last chapter, Jim wrote *In Good Company: The Fast Track from the Corporate World to Poverty, Chastity and Obedience* while in Nairobi, sick with mononucleosis, in early 1993. He was supposed to be resting, but took the time to write. The subtitle was of his own choosing. He knew what would catch readers' attention. While it was written in 1993, the book did not appear until 2000.

In 2010, Jim wrote in the introduction to a tenth anniversary edition: "[I]f someone had asked what led me to enter the Jesuits, I would have answered like this: I was miserable in my job and discovered a lifeline, a wonderful new way to live. And that's true. God offered me a way out. Now, however, I would describe things using a more overtly spiritual vocabulary. What happened to me is what happens in all 'vocation' stories: God called me through desire."[17]

Several years after that, when I asked him how the original 1993 draft might have differed from the published version, Jim explained: "I was much more judgmental when I [first] wrote it. . . . When I reread it a few years later, after returning from Nairobi, I realized how judgmental it was and changed it." He also reflected on his negative perceptions about the corporate world, which come through clearly in the memoir, based on his experiences. "Later I came to see that business could be a real vocation for people."[18]

Soon he was giving retreats and talks and writing articles on how to live a spiritual life in the corporate world. One notices, reading of Jim's departure from the world of business as depicted in his memoir, that, after six years of earning well at General Electric, he seems to have owned relatively little. He also tells the reader that when he entered the Jesuits he was a virgin. So did the vows of a Jesuit feel like much of a challenge to him? I asked him. "Not at the time, because I didn't really understand them. I never was much for owning things: my biggest purchase was a car, but then again, I was still young. I gave my parents I think $25,000 to hold onto in case I left the Jesuits. But they ended up needing to use most of it in a few years," he said.[19]

In Good Company was a story tailor-made for intriguing secular media. Why would anyone with "a large office, a private secretary and an enviable salary" (that's how a *Wall Street Journal* profile described it) decide to go to seminary and become a priest? And the large photograph of Jim accompanying the profile, which was subtitled "Record Numbers of People Enter Clergy as Second Career; From Briefcases to

Bibles," showed him in a collar talking to a police officer on the street. The caption: "Ex-secular: Father James Martin, a former human-resources executive, near ground zero [*sic*]."[20] Then came a feature in "The Buzz" section of *Workforce* magazine, which concluded: "And corporate HR can learn a lot from the Jesuits, [Martin] adds. The most important lesson: 'to treat each person with dignity.' "[21]

In Good Company appealed to the large audience of working Americans dissatisfied with what they do, seeking something more meaningful. Another review—again in the *Wall Street Journal*, above the fold in the Sunday Business section, with a four-inch-tall image of the book and a six-inch-tall head shot of the author—included two headlines: "Jesuitry at GE?" followed by, "For one GE refugee, redemption meant joining the Society of Jesus."[22]

A month later, a full page by "The Rev. James Martin, a member of the Society of Jesus and a Plymouth Meeting native," appeared in the *Philadelphia Inquirer*. It included an impressive photograph taken by an *Inquirer* photographer of Jim in his blacks and collar at the Times Square subway platform, as well as this conversation Jim had with a stranger on Track 3 in Thirtieth Street Station in Philadelphia. She had been eyeing him in his clerics:

> "So," she says, "is that, like, a costume?"
> "No," I say. "Does it look like a costume?"
> "Oh yeah," she says, pushing away a stray blond hair. "It's definitely a costume."
> "Which part?"
> "Oh, please," she laughs. "The whole thing!"

By this time, Jim had been wearing a collar for two years, and he felt about the priesthood, as he liked to quote from Thomas Merton, as "the one great secret for which I was born."[23]

* * *

From the experience at GE, he'd retained a savvy understanding of business and markets, and now he was applying
it to his work as a journalist, author, and priest. As he had
explained years earlier, he understood: "Madison Avenue's
tack seems to be this: Spirituality is hot. Why? Well, appar-
ently, after a decade of working weekends, baby boomers
and yuppies have discovered that careers and money aren't
everything."[24]

He would return to this theme again and again. For example, beginning a December article in *America* with "It's
beginning to look a lot like Christmas. And it's starting to
bug me just a little bit," he goes on to take to task the con-
sumerist exploitation of the incarnation by J.C. Penney, Eddie
Bauer, Land's End, and Macy's department stores, saying, "I
know this is the way marketing works, using anything to
hawk a product. And I'm sorry to be a stickler, but it's strange
seeing the Christian faith being used and denied at the same
time."[25] The same article, in slightly different form, appeared
two days earlier in the *Wall Street Journal*.

At *America*, Jim was a delight to his editor in chief. "I
wish I could have cloned him," Tom Reese said.

Jim first appeared on television because Reese would frequently receive phone calls from producers seeking someone
to comment on a story, show, film, or media controversy. In
the late nineties, Reese began sending some of them Jim's
way, in a conscious effort to raise the magazine's profile and
to help Jim gain exposure.

"I always considered working with media as part of our
ministry," Reese said. "It was also good for the magazine
because the more we got our name out there, the more
subscriptions we sold. Whenever I thought he was more

knowledgeable on the topic, I would refer journalists to him. For example, he had written great articles on Opus Dei, anti-Catholicism, and homosexuality. Whenever I got calls on these topics, I would refer the reporters to Jim." The referrals came with an elder's advice, particularly in those days when there were watchdogs in Vatican City keeping an eye on liberal American priests and theologians. Reese remembers: "I did coach him a little. For example, on some controversial topics, I warned him to avoid giving his own opinion. Better to say, 'some theologians say this . . . , some say that . . . , the pope says this . . .' I did not want him getting into trouble."[26]

After appearances on CNN and Fox News came *The O'Reilly Factor*, hosted by the controversial political commentator and personality Bill O'Reilly. Jim remembers:

> Tom and I would watch some of my appearances and he would give me pointers, which were very helpful. Like if someone is saying something terrible about the church and you're listening and nodding (which I sometimes do when I'm listening) stop nodding since it looks like you're agreeing. Tom actually said, "When Bill O'Reilly is saying that all the bishops should be in jail, you should probably stop nodding."[27]

He was often being quoted in national media with the descriptor, "Jesuit TV columnist" or "Jesuit culture commentator" after his name.

* * *

With newfound celebrity came unpleasant responsibility. In March 2002, Jim appeared for the first time on the op-ed page of the *New York Times* addressing the role of celibacy in priestly life and how it relates, or doesn't, to what was then a growing pedophilia scandal. The *Boston Globe*'s Spotlight investigative team had published its first article, "Church Allowed Abuse by Priest for Years" in its January 6, 2002, edition. Sharing the opinion page that day in March were William Safire and Witold Rybczynski—famous company to keep.

Jim was writing to explain the tradition of celibacy, arguing that there is no connection between a vow of celibacy and a tendency toward criminal sexual behavior: "The criminal acts of a few do not negate the value of celibacy, any more than spousal abuse or incest can negate the value of marriage or marital love."[28] A day earlier, the always provocative, once-Jesuit Garry Wills had written in *The Boston Globe Magazine*, "The whole celibacy structure is a house of cards, and honesty about any one problem can make the structure of pretense come toppling down. . . . Treating pedophilia as a separate problem is impossible, since it thrives by its place in a compromised network of evasion."[29]

Jim was also disputing the conclusions of A. W. Richard Sipe, a former-priest-turned-psychotherapist who was researching to discover causes of clergy sex abuse and who was quoted by the Spotlight team in Boston. Sipe's work began in the 1980s and was delivered even to the US Conference of Catholic Bishops during that decade. He was also a frequent expert witness for the prosecution in civil cases brought by abused plaintiffs against the church. (His work was revealed later to a larger audience when he was a minor character in the 2015 film, *Spotlight*, winner of the Academy Award for Best Picture, about the *Globe*'s investigations of the crisis in the Archdiocese of Boston.) Sipe's conclusions included findings that 6 percent of priests were sexual abusers of minors at one time or another and that as few as half of all priests were living faithfully to their celibacy vows.

Martin made no mention of Sipe in his op-ed, but the argument against celibacy was not over. It has resurfaced often, every time the scandal returns.

For example, in early 2005, an increasingly popular website for young Catholics and former Catholics, BustedHalo, published a four-part interview with a closeted gay priest who'd written an article for *Commonweal* under the pseudonym, Fr. Gerard Thomas, saying that the Vatican should not, as it was rumored to be contemplating, issue any document forbidding homosexual men from the priesthood. The anonymous priest, in the final portion of the interview, said:

> [M]y fears regarding the Vatican issuing this document that bars or restricts the ordination of gay priests is that it is going to drive the healthy discussion of sexuality and homosexuality further underground. . . . You're saying to someone we want you to be celibate or chaste but we never want you to talk about your sexuality. How can that person come to a healthy understanding of what it means to be celibate and chaste? I think it's impossible.[30]

Fr. Gerard seemed to be siding with Sipe.

At the end of August that year (2005), Pope Benedict XVI approved a document that was published in November: "Instruction Concerning the Criteria for the Discernment of Vocations with Regard to Persons with Homosexual Tendencies in View of Their Admission to the Seminary and to Holy Orders." It included:

> The Church, while profoundly respecting the persons in question [so-called "persons with homosexual tendencies"], cannot admit to the seminary or to holy orders those who practice homosexuality, present deep-seated homosexual tendencies or support the so-called "gay culture."[31]

* * *

Meanwhile, Jim's articles were being quoted by other journalists, and Jim was being asked to comment more and more on television and other national and international media.

By early 2004, he was writing in *Newsday* about Mel Gibson's controversial blockbuster film, *The Passion of the Christ*. "I found 'The Passion of the Christ' in many places anti-Semitic and in most places simply repellent," he wrote on the film's opening day (Ash Wednesday). Most of all, Jim's point was communicated in the title of his review: "If only Gibson had shown the death and the life."

Gibson's film infamously portrayed the shocking bloodiness of the lynching of Christ; Jim concluded: "I was left depressed . . . in response to the film's brutally graphic portrayal of the Passion," and "for [the lost] chance to reflect not simply on the last 12 hours of the life of Jesus, but on the years before he climbed the hill at Calvary."[32] Even despite such reservations, Gibson's film earned nearly 84 million dollars at the box office that opening weekend.

Less than two weeks later Jim was on the opinion page of the *New York Sun* on the subject of "Keeping the collar through the crisis." He set out to answer the question, Why do you stay in the Catholic Church and remain a priest amid a sex abuse crisis? Answers ranged from faithfulness to his vows, understanding that scandal and sin in the church is nothing new, and "[t]here are some signs that penance and reconciliation . . . have already begun." He would answer the same question in similar ways many times in decades to come.

In another opinion piece, he addressed the scandal with words that would turn out to be prescient: "The sexual abuse crisis is not over. . . . [U]ntil one of the central mandates of the Second Vatican Council is implemented—when bishops and priests are ready to cede some of their power and lay-persons are able to assume leadership roles—the way out will lead only to more frustration, confusion and sadness."[33]

Jim also shared more personally why he remains: "I love being a priest and believe that it is where I am meant to be. It is a privilege to celebrate Mass, hear confessions, marry couples, baptize children and anoint the sick."[34]

CHAPTER FOUR

Looking to the Saints

It took Jim twenty-one years to become a "fully professed" Jesuit, an extraordinarily long amount of time, by any standard, to fulfill a professional goal or earn a degree. But twenty-one years is not uncommon in the Society of Jesus. Following his two years in the novitiate, and taking his simple vows, he did his First Studies, followed by three years of full-time work during what Jesuits call regency. This was his time in East Africa, plus the first year at *America*. Then came theology studies in Harvard Square, followed by ordination, followed by working full time at *America*. All that was left, then, were his Final Vows. One constancy throughout that time was a growing devotion to, and education in, the saints.

His earliest published writings were preoccupied with saints and a life in pursuit of holiness, in the style that he would later became famous for. There was an article in 1993 for *Review for Religious* titled "Hope in Loneliness," written from Nairobi and speaking personally about his sadness there, quoting his favorite noncanonized saint, Thomas Merton, and the recently canonized Claude de la Colombière, SJ, who said that only Jesus Christ can ultimately satisfy the heart. "So I suppose that saints are people who, like Claude, recognize this mystery and do not fear the prospect of being alone," Jim concluded.[1]

A few months later, his first article for a large circulation magazine appeared in *Catholic Digest*. They condensed a piece he'd written a year earlier for the *National Jesuit News* titled "Rescuing St. Al." Jim was already finding ways to say that spiritual heroes and saints were ordinary people doing extraordinary things. He took to task popular images that make saints appear weak or even effeminate:

> Aloysius Gonzaga, for example, as a young man carried plague victims to the hospitals in Rome. Usually, he is pictured as a delicate child.

He goes on to criticize "saccharine hagiography"—showing an early ability to speak to ordinary people when referring to a book on Jesuit saints and martyrs as being "mercifully free of goopy language"—as well as misleading iconography. He appeals for honest, accurate investigations of the lives of saints, who were real people doing real things. He praises images that are on target, such as: "[A] friend once gave me a drawing by William Hart McNichols of St. Aloysius with a child in his arms. Next to him is a boy with a black eye, and there's a small girl with a torn dress, hiding behind his torn cassock. That's St. Aloysius."[2]

* * *

For a priest and writer so closely associated now with the saints, Jim found them in life rather late. As he explained to me:

The world that I grew up in was not one in which the saints figured at all. We prayed to St. Anthony when we lost things in our family. We took a saint's name at confirmation (and even then I was taking my grandfather's name, not in any honor of St. Thomas) and we celebrated St. Patrick's Day since my dad's family was Irish. But as for knowing the stories of the saints, praying to them, or talking about them, that was not done. Mainly because my parents, while good Catholics, were not super-religious. It's always been something of a mystery to me, especially since my mother was first-generation Italian, and my father second-generation Irish, both ethnic groups whose members often have a strong devotional life. But I suppose their parents weren't that religious either, or at least didn't talk about the saints all that much.

He went on:

It's also odd because my dad went to West Catholic High School, run by the LaSalle Christian Brothers. So my mom comes from a Sicilian family (literally: both of her parents were off-the-boat immigrants) and my dad goes to a Catholic high school and comes from an Irish family. My only thought was that they were both trying to be more "American" at a time when being either Irish or Italian still could engender some stereotyping. My mom once told me that they decided not to name my sister and me "Italian" names because of a desire to avoid prejudice.[3]

In his first twenty-six years, the only saint that had meaning for him personally was St. Jude—in the form of a nine-inch mail-order statue he sent away for, spurred by a magazine advertisement—a humorous story he tells in the introduction to *My Life with the Saints*. (He also tells it in *In Good Company*.)

After what was a feeble experience with St. Jude, appealing to the statue on his knees in hopes of excelling on big exams and the like, then hiding Jude away in a sock drawer, Jim returns to his account in *My Life* of encountering Thomas Merton on television while still a young executive at GE, exhausted at the end of a long day. It was that documentary of Merton that started his saint-clock ticking. Jim would say, from that moment on, that Merton was cheering him on, helping him discover who he was to become.

First, he became a Jesuit—"certainly the best decision I've ever made," he has said on many occasions. Then, inspired (or provoked) by listening to fellow Jesuits talk about "their" saints, he began to reconsider what saints were all about. He was quite Protestant, in fact, in his views on saints at that time. "I . . . found the idea of praying to the saints wholly superstitious. What was the point? If God hears your prayers, why do you need the saints?"[4]

But he learned quickly, and he found many saints cheering him on—enough to write his biggest book to date about them.

My Life with the Saints began with a different title. Pat Kossmann, the former book editor who had become *America*'s literary editor, took one look at the manuscript, titled by Jim *Holy in a Different Way: My Life with the Saints*, and said, "Your subtitle is your real title." The book was already in production at the publisher, but Jim asked if they would change the title. So they did.

He'd become an excellent memoirist: honest, vulnerable, humorous, inspiring. Stretching his writing legs, so to speak, over four hundred pages he describes how he started from a place of skepticism and thereby won many hearts to the subject. Chapters focus on the canonized and the not-quite-canonized: Joan of Arc, Thérèse of Lisieux, Thomas Merton,

Ignatius of Loyola, Pedro Arrupe, Bernadette Soubirous, Mother Teresa, Pope John XXIII, Dorothy Day, St. Peter, Thomas Aquinas, Francis of Assisi, St. Joseph, the Ugandan Martyrs, Aloysius Gonzaga, and the Blessed Virgin Mary. His conclusion is stated also in the introduction, and he'd learned it first from Merton:

> I realized that none of us are meant to be Thérèse of Lisieux or Pope John XXIII or Thomas More. We're meant to be ourselves, and meant to allow God to work in and through our own individuality, our own humanity.

* * *

My Life with the Saints was published on Ash Wednesday, March 1, 2006. It was the book that changed Jim's career as an author—his "breakout."

The day before the release, Shrove Tuesday, Jim was a guest on National Public Radio's *All Things Considered*, talking about the practice of giving things up for Lent. His Jewish friend Rob has, since college, called him on Ash Wednesday to tell him what to give up for forty days. This began as a dare among friends at Doc Watson's bar one night in college, then became part of Jim's spiritual practice. The show finished the interview, quoting Jim saying: "When I was dealing with a long illness, I once complained to an older priest that I didn't want that particular cross. He said, well it wouldn't be much of a cross if you wanted it, would it? . . . Last year I told Rob I was worried that one day he was going to assign something really hard to give up. It was like worrying about God asking me to sacrifice something. Another reason to stay on my good side, said Rob, and on God's good side, too."[5]

My Life with the Saints won the Christopher Award and was named the best hardcover spirituality book of that year by the Catholic Press Association. Then there were spinoffs: an audiobook read by the author; a DVD, *Who Cares about the Saints?*, popular with teenagers and parish groups; and an unabridged Spanish translation, *Mi vida con los santos*. (It has since been published in several other languages.) But the success started slowly. It took eighteen months to find the audience; then, it turned out, the audience was huge and beyond the walls of churches. Suddenly Jim was being interviewed everywhere and writing about saints everywhere. A small sampling of his articles, and their opening lines, illustrates the point:

The New York Times op-ed page:	"Last month, while Americans celebrated the feast of two secular saints, George Washington and Abraham Lincoln, the Vatican issued a surprising new directive calling for greater rigor in its own saint-making process . . ."
The Wall Street Journal:	"After their wedding in Alençon, France, on July 13, 1858, Louis Martin and Zélie Guerin refrained from sex for 10 months."
Slate Magazine:	"Christmas cards tend to fall into three categories. . . . But where's St. Joseph? . . . He's off to the side or stuck in the back, behind a shepherd."[6]

He had established himself as an accessible, intelligent, articulate, and good-humored media source. Religion reporters (of which there were still a goodly number) relied on him as an engaging explainer of American Catholicism. The book received extensive media coverage. In addition to the reviews and coverage, Jim did a commentary for NPR's *All Things Considered*, appeared on Fox News's *The O'Reilly Factor* and CNN's Sunday morning faith segment, and was interviewed by *USA Today*, the *Philadelphia Inquirer*, *Boston Globe*, and Religion News Service, among others. He was sought for a *Time* magazine feature in which he was asked to comment on Raul Castro saying that Fidel was "protected by the socialist saints" (with the tongue-in-cheek headline "Oh, When the Lefty Saints Go Marching In").

It also didn't hurt that he was then able to enlist endorsements from cardinals in the church, Vatican journalists, other bestselling authors, and theologians. The early "blurbers" and reviewers included Avery Cardinal Dulles, SJ, Lawrence S. Cunningham of the University of Notre Dame, novelist Ron Hansen, and *National Catholic Reporter*'s journalist in Rome, John L. Allen Jr. (who wrote the foreword).

And his publisher was savvy. Publicist Kelly Hughes remembers:

> As the initial launch was winding down, one of the brilliant minds at Loyola Press had the idea for a "Use Your Common Saints" campaign, pointing motorists to the saints for help handling their daily commutes. Banners featuring messages from St. Jude, St. Anthony, Joan of Arc, and St. Joseph reminded drivers of the virtues of patience and good humor. The banners were hung from the back of St. Stanislaus Kostka Church, which abuts the Kennedy expressway at about 1300 North. Each saint's message was up for two weeks. "St. Jude knows an alternate route"; "St. Joseph says construction takes patience"; "St. Ignatius encourages Mass transit"; "Joan of Arc says keep your cool"; "St. Anthony offers roadside assistance." The media response was terrific, both here in Chicago and nationwide. Jim was on Chicago Public Radio, WLS-TV (ABC) Ch. 7 News did a story, the *Tribune* and *Sun-Times* covered it, and an RNS story was picked up all over the country, among others.[7]

When the US economy almost collapsed in October 2008, after Goldman Sachs and Morgan Stanley nearly went belly-up, the US Congress passed the Emergency Economic Stabilization Act. Jim was quoted by *Time* magazine in an article titled, "Is It OK to Pray for Your 401(k)?" He said: "People absolutely need to know that it's natural to ask God's help in times of crisis." *My Life with the Saints* sold fifty thousand copies in the first twenty-two months, most of those after the eighteen-month mark. The number increased to one hundred thousand after forty-eight months, by March 2010.

He was soon writing for *O, The Oprah Magazine*, in praise of the fifty-nine thousand religious sisters who announced their support for a healthcare reform bill in Congress that the US Catholic bishops had officially opposed. And he wasn't averse to using his new position of influence to come to the aid of a friend, writing to the editor of the *New York Times Book Review* responding to a negative review of his friend Paul Mariani's new biography of Gerard Manley Hopkins. Reviewer Blake Bailey had criticized Mariani for skirting sexuality issues in the life of the priest-poet. Bailey, Jim says, "misses what Hopkins might call the 'forestfromthetrees.' . . . Over all, it is a splendid book, and the lack of emphasis on sexuality detracts very little from what I would count as the first mainstream biography that presents Hopkins as he would probably describe himself: a Jesuit first, a poet second."[8]

Most important, for Jim, writing *My Life with the Saints* taught him an important life lesson. As he recently explained to me:

> I learned that Thomas Merton was right when he wrote, "For me to be a saint means to be myself." I started the

book thinking it would be fun to write about the saints that I felt so devoted to. But as I wrote, I started to realize, on a deep level, just how true that Merton quote was. The saints really *were* very different from one another, sometimes completely different. And that helped me to realize that I really am called to be myself—no more but, more importantly, no less. It has also helped me with people who come for spiritual direction, especially younger Jesuits who (like all of us) sometimes have a tendency to compare themselves to one another.

A few years earlier, one of my Jesuit superiors, with the best intentions, insisted that I needed to get a PhD, when I was almost forty and not interested in any more studies. So I said that I didn't feel called to that. He himself was an academic, and kept pushing and finally told me how disappointed he was in me for not pursuing a doctorate. Years later, I wondered if he believed that people were truly called to be who they are. Meaning, I wondered if he thought that everyone needs to get a PhD. But for me Merton's statement is fundamental. Your path to holiness is your own. It's been tremendously helpful in ministry, too. I often tell people, "God is not calling Mother Teresa or Pope Francis to your ministry, so stop wondering what they would do in your place. God has placed you in that situation. The better question is what *you* would do."[9]

Becoming who you are meant to become became Jim's focus in nearly every aspect of his ministry. Later that year, in September 2006, he published another book that has had an impact on many people: *Becoming Who You Are: Insights on the True Self from Thomas Merton and Other Saints*.

In many respects, *Becoming Who You Are* is Jim's most signal, representative work, explaining his full view of the Christian life. The first sentence quotes from Merton, from *New Seeds of Contemplation*, and summarizes Jim's approach to living his own faith: "For me to be a saint means to be myself." Discovering one's true self, then, is central to becoming a follower of Christ. Every disciple is unique, and not until the task of discovering one's uniqueness, one's gifts, learning to become who you are, is undertaken, does one become a true disciple.

It could be said that this is the Gospel according to James Martin.

* * *

On November 1, 2009, Jim professed his Final Vows as a Jesuit. In the formal letter to his provincial one year earlier, he had said, "[I]t is with immense joy that I request this final incorporation into the Society of Jesus. After twenty years as a Jesuit, and almost ten as a priest, I can say wholeheartedly, without reservation, and with abundant gratitude that I feel called, and confirmed, in this most wonderful gift from God: my vocation as a Jesuit."[10]

In his homily that day, at the eleven o'clock morning Solemn Mass at St. Ignatius Church, he preached:

> Lately I've realized something about Christianity. . . . It's hard. . . . When I entered the Jesuits I figured that if I really understood the Gospel, prayed hard and got my act together—spiritually, psychologically, emotionally—I could live the Christian life with ease. . . . But that's not true at all. It's an effort. It takes work. It's hard. Forgiving people is hard. Loving is hard. . . . Working with the poor can be frightening. Caring for someone who is ill can be scary. And you start to doubt that you'll make it. You think, "I'll never be able to do this. I'll never be able to climb this far." But you can. You can with the help of friends, who urge you on, saying, "Come on, just a little further." You can climb that ladder, within the church. You can walk towards Jesus.

He was a priest without any sense of clericalism. Nodding to his family and friends who were there to celebrate with him that day, he was preaching the way that readers had come to expect in his honest writing.

By this point the Church of St. Ignatius Loyola, one of two Jesuit churches in Manhattan, had become a central part of his spiritual life. Many of those who know Jim only as a "famous priest" may have little understanding of his regular priestly duties. Since his ordination to the priesthood in 1999, he has celebrated Sunday Mass on a regular basis at St. Ignatius and participates in the rest of the liturgical year in the parish, joining his brother priests for celebration of the Easter Triduum and Midnight Mass at Christmas, among other events.

He was also by this point in great demand as a spiritual director, helping others find God in their prayer and their daily lives. A few years before Final Vows, he participated in a summer-long spiritual direction training program at the Jesuit Spiritual Center in Milford, Ohio, under the tutelage of two experienced directors. The program honed his skills as a director and also provided him with his first opportunity to direct people in the full Ignatian Spiritual Exercises. After completing the program, his regular "directees" in New York City ranged from young Jesuits in First Studies at Fordham University, to St. Ignatius parishioners, to young men discerning a vocation to the Jesuits, to men and women who sought Jim out after reading one of his books. Jim would meet with them in the evenings or on weekends at his Jesuit community, usually for an hour monthly. At one point he had as many as ten directees.

Most of these more "spiritual duties" (including the baptisms, weddings, and funerals that are the duties of all priests, and Masses at his own Jesuit community), not to mention his own regular life of prayer and making his own annual retreats, were probably not as well known by those who only knew Jim from his books, articles, and media appearances.

He was indeed famous by then, at least as much as a writer of religious books can be. And by the time of his Final Vows, Jim had also begun to earn a great deal of money for the Society of Jesus by his writing. He had one experience, soon before professing those Final Vows, of receiving a royalty check of about $200,000 from the publisher of *My Life with the Saints*, knowing that he would keep none of it for himself. He did not mind.

Bestsellers in an author's past mean large advances (royalties paid upfront, by contract) and generous royalty rates for future projects. To this day, Jim earns advances of $100,000 or so, and he's likely earned more than three million dollars for America Media over the decades from his various books. This does not include the revenue his publishers have paid to advertise his books in the pages of *America*; often, two to three pages per issue have been taken up by such ads.

For the curious: Since Jim works in a "writer's house"— a technical Jesuit term—his income goes there. (Other Jesuit authors see their royalties go to their Provinces.) Stipends for Jim's speeches are split equally between America Media and America House, his Jesuit community. More specifically, those speeches he gives during the week that take him away from his "day job" go to America Media, and the ones that take place on a weekend and nearby in the evenings go to his community. All this flows from his vow of poverty.

Those are just details, however. One only has to read a paragraph from one of his books to see that Jim writes from love for the work, for God, and in ministry to others.

CHAPTER FIVE

Going to the Theater

Heretical as it is for someone living in New York,
I must confess: I almost never go to the theater.

James Martin, SJ, February 12, 2000[1]

What a difference a few years can make. Jim went from
television reviewer ("low culture") to theater ("high culture") consultant in the first decade of the twenty-first century. In the quote that heads this chapter, taken from one of
his "Of Many Things" articles, he tongue-in-cheek confesses
to not being much of a theatergoer. Actually, he takes the
first half of that column to apologize for going to a show.
Listing reasons why he doesn't, or shouldn't—most of all,
"have you checked the price of a Broadway ticket lately?
Not at all doable on a slim Jesuit stipend"—he says that a
complimentary pass to a play called *Siciliano* allowed him
to attend.

One month later, he had a cover story in *America* on the
subject of anti-Catholicism in American life ("The Last Acceptable Prejudice?") and stated: "[T]he entertainment industry is where one finds the most obvious contempt for the

Catholic Church. It is as if producers, directors, playwrights and filmmakers feel obliged to establish their intellectual bona fides by trumpeting their differences."[2]

There were also other times when Jim wasn't an easy reviewer of playwrights and actors. He once pointed to New York's most well-regarded playwright at the time, Tony Kushner, taking him to task for writing in *The Nation* and calling Pope John Paul II "a homicidal liar" who "endorses murder."[3]

But Jim would soon show his openness to transformation through the experience of theater.

* * *

The Last Days of Judas Iscariot, written by Stephen Adly Guirgis, tells the story of the infamous apostle having his day in court, after death, in heaven. Guirgis, who would later go on to win a Pulitzer Prize, seeks to consider whether the man who betrayed Jesus should have been so summarily convicted by the court of opinion.

Off-Broadway productions often don't receive much media attention, but this one, which played at the Public Theater, was different. A young Philip Seymour Hoffman—fresh off his Oscar-winning role in *Capote*—directed, and Sam Rockwell starred as Judas. The characters of Mother Teresa, Sigmund Freud, Pontius Pilate, and Satan were all called to the stand to "testify."

Guirgis, whose interest in Judas began as a child in Catholic school in New York City, described himself as a "confused, often irate and disconsolate lapsed Catholic" while working with Jim.[4] A respected playwright with a reputation for curse-laden monologues, he had St. Monica, the mother of St. Augustine, swearing on stage in act 1, scene 1. To any Catholic, this would seem, to say the least, out of character for her. Perhaps most interesting of all, actor Eric Bogosian played Satan and was thought by many to have stolen the show with his performance.

Jim was first approached in late October 2004 by Sam Rockwell, who left a message on his voicemail. "I'm an actor who is working on a play about Judas. Would you be willing to talk with me about him?" At first, it seemed that Jim's work would be only with Guirgis and Rockwell, but he ended up acting as a theological adviser to the cast, crew, director, and playwright and was interviewed in the media throughout the run of the play.

Guirgis described his working relationship, which turned into a friendship, with the Jesuit:

> Have you ever wanted to cross-examine a Priest? I did. Over many lunches and dinners and coffees and late-night phone calls and even later-night calls, and then during early-morning meetings after late-night dinners and phone calls, I forcefully, aggressively, and desperately cross-examined Father Jim on anything and everything having to do with Scripture, Catholicism and Jesus.[5]

Jim introduced everyone to books, articles, and ideas on issues of the historical Jesus, first-century Palestine, theodicy, despair, and faith. He answered questions and then posed other questions, always seeking to deepen the exploration of the themes at play in the provocative production. Jim has always been a good student, even long after classes are over: keeping notes, remembering key points, quoting his instructors. This he did in abundance. There were many passionate discussions over a six-month period—over meals, during rehearsals, and, as Guirgis noted, even late at night on the telephone. Jim describes one of them:

"Why couldn't God just break through [Judas's] despair?"
Stephen asked.

Frustrated, I shouted into the phone: "No! That's not
the way it works! You have to participate in your own
salvation!"

The next day, one of the Jesuits in my community asked,
horrified, "Who were you shouting at last night? That's no
way to talk to someone in despair!"[6]

Readings for the play began in early January 2005; pre-
views started February 8, continuing for two weeks; opening night was March 2; and the show closed on April 3 after
a mostly sold-out run. Jim was quoted in a full-page *Time
Out New York* article about his role in the production and
his admiration for the process: "It was really fascinating to
come to rehearsals. Phil [Seymour Hoffman] came up with
several parables from his life to illustrate poverty of spirit
for the actors. And I thought, How interesting: That's what
Jesus did."[7]

Three years later, *The Last Days of Judas Iscariot* had
another six-week run, with a different cast and director, in
London's West End.

A Jesuit Off-Broadway, Jim's account of the experience
of working on the production, getting to know the actors,
director, and crew, delving into the characters of Judas and
Jesus and many other aspects of first-century life and theology, was published September 1, 2007. *My Life with the
Saints* was still in active promotion, itself only eighteen
months old. For that reason, some of Jim's audience of readers missed this interesting episode in his life altogether.

He would, in 2007, once again work as an adviser to
Philip Seymour Hoffman, this time on a film costarring
Meryl Streep: *Doubt*, by another remarkable twentieth-
century writer, John Patrick Shanley, adapted from his own

play. Hoffman played a priest accused of sexual abuse of a child. This is a hot topic in any era but particularly in that first decade of the twenty-first century, just after the *Boston Globe* broke the story wide open through its Spotlight investigative team. It was put to Jim to help Hoffman understand what it would have felt like to be a priest so accused and likely guilty.

The film was set in the Bronx in 1964, in the Catholic atmosphere immediately before the impact of Second Vatican Council reforms. Jim said:

> We spent a good deal of time talking about what it meant to be a priest, going to Masses at St. Ignatius Loyola Church in New York, and even spending time practicing celebrating Mass. (After one Mass, I took him up on the high altar so that he could get a sense of what the priest would have seen in the early 1960s.)[8]

Doubt was released on Christmas Day 2008. It was nominated for five Academy Awards, including Hoffman for Best Supporting Actor. (On a far sadder note, Jim would also celebrate Hoffman's Funeral Mass at St. Ignatius Church in 2014.)

Jim spent much less time on the set of *Doubt* than he did at *The Last Days of Judas Iscariot*. In an interview, he once described the experience of both projects, saying, "John Courtney Murray, the Jesuit priest, used to say that the Jesuits' role is to explain the Church to the world and the world to the Church. So this is mostly explaining the Church to the world."[9]

He would have at least a few more turns at theater and Hollywood in the years to come.

* * *

There were other motivations to be out of the office during the time of *The Last Days of Judas Iscariot*. The year 2005 was tumultuous at *America* magazine, perhaps one reason why Jim enjoyed his time away. Editor in chief Tom Reese was engaged in an on-again off-again intrareligious battle with the Congregation for the Doctrine of the Faith and its prefect, Cardinal Joseph Ratzinger, over several editorials and articles that struck a persistently critical tone of the church.

The congregation's concerns had first become known to Reese in April 2002 and included Jim's November 2000 article, "The Church and the Homosexual Priest," among others.[10] Jim remembers: "[They] said that if we didn't accede to their requests, they would either fire Tom or put in place a board of ecclesiastical censors. So we tried to be a bit less controversial, and eventually we were told that our time of trial was over, and that we were in the clear. That's why the firing of Tom was so surprising."[11]

On May 6, *National Catholic Reporter* broke the story that Reese had resigned. The following day, media outlets all over the world reported similarly to what one found in the *Los Angeles Times*:

> Father Thomas Reese, a widely known Catholic writer and pundit, has resigned as editor of the Jesuit magazine *America* under pressure from a Vatican congregation once headed by Pope Benedict XVI. Reese's decisions to publish articles that at times challenged the church's official views brought Vatican criticism. His resignation followed several years of exchanges among the magazine, Reese's superiors in the Society of Jesus, known as the Jesuits, and the Vatican's Congregation for the Doctrine of the Faith.[12]

After years of rancor, it was a letter from the Vatican to Peter-Hans Kolvenbach, SJ, the Society of Jesus' superior general in Rome, that precipitated Reese's resignation. Cardinal Ratzinger had asked Father Kolvenbach for Reese's removal. The letter was sent in March, just before the death of Pope John Paul II, and it circulated quickly among the Jesuit Curia. Reese probably never even saw it, but, as the *L.A. Times* reported, "Kolvenbach relayed the contents . . . to the president of the Jesuit conference in the U.S., Father Brad Schaeffer, who then informed Reese. 'What it [the letter] amounted to is that it wasn't going to do any good to fight this. The sense was that Reese had to go,' one source told *The Times*."

Then, John Paul II died, and a papal conclave was called. Reese was in Rome covering that conclave. When Cardinal Ratzinger was elected as the next pope, on April 19, 2005, Reese returned to the States immediately, knowing how complicated his situation now was, with someone who disapproved of his leadership of the magazine now pope.

One month later, when Jim wrote his next "Of Many Things" column, it was about Reese's departure—not the politics of it, but how Reese would be missed. He slyly inserted this in the second paragraph:

> He will be sorely missed, then, not simply by the editors, staff and readers of America magazine, but by legions of journalists, quite literally across the world. A few days after the announcement of Tom's resignation, Archbishop William Levada was appointed prefect of the Congregation for the Doctrine of the Faith. A religion reporter from a small-town paper called me and said, "Who will explain these things to me now?"[13]

When Reese had returned home from Rome, initially he offered to resign, but the other editors (at that point unaware of the instructions from the then-Cardinal Ratzinger and now Benedict XVI) told him to think more carefully about it. "Don't make a decision in a time of uncertainty," as St. Ignatius would say. So, Reese decided to stay on. But a few days later, word came down from Jesuit headquarters that he was being ordered to resign. "We had a rather dramatic meeting where this was announced, and we all wondered: Can you have a 'journal of opinion' if you're not allowed to have an opinion?" recalls Jim.[14]

Reese, fully obedient, left.

America's remaining editorial staff went through gymnastics of emotion. Briefly, they considered shutting the magazine down. When those feelings passed, Jim then thought for a short while that he might want to be editor in chief. He thought he'd be good at it, also that it made sense in the arc of his "career." This too passed, when Jim (and his superiors, the ones to make such decisions) realized he was best suited to writing and all the other things he does as an associate editor (later, "editor at large").

America soon found its new leadership in Drew Christiansen, SJ, an experienced moral theologian who was seen by many as Tom Reese's clear "heir apparent." And thanks to Christiansen's long experience with the hierarchy (he had worked at the United States Conference of Catholic Bishops), he was able to restore the magazine to the good graces of the ecclesial leadership in both the United States and the Vatican.

* * *

Jim managed to publish one more book that year (2005), an edited collection of essays on liturgy that had all appeared in the pages of *America*.

Celebrating Good Liturgy: A Guide to the Ministries of the Mass was simple for someone of Jim's talents to produce, but it also demonstrated his ongoing interest in priestly congregational work. Presiding at Mass, preparing homilies, and articulating the value of the sacraments with people remained essential to his life, as they still do today. Jim concluded his introduction (his only written part of the book) in July 2005:

> After collecting and editing these essays, I noticed that not only did I celebrate Mass a little differently (and better, I hope!) but also that, to paraphrase Vatican II, I more fully and actively understood the value of everyone's ministry. All of this added to my appreciation of the church's great sacrament.[15]

CHAPTER SIX

More Bad Priests, Ignatian Practices, and Joy

The life of every Catholic priest in America in the late twentieth and early twenty-first centuries has been marked in some way by the clergy sex-abuse scandals. Given his position in the media and renown in the public eye, when the crisis reached its first boiling point Jim was asked by national and international media to comment. Doing so was at times nearly a full-time job.

Even back in the spring of 1995, he seemed weary of the responsibility, writing about an invitation from Miramax to screen a new film about a priest and his troubles: "Finally, I thought, a movie about priests who weren't molesting children." He attended the screening and then spoke and wrote somewhat favorably about the film. To his surprise, he then ended up in controversy when the Catholic League condemned it. After being interviewed by New York Newsday, CBS-TV, and others, Jim reflected in *America*, "I realized once again the inability of sound-bite driven television to explain adequately the nuances of religion. There was no way anyone could coherently elucidate the value of celibacy in 10 seconds. It also became clear that it was in TV's interest to frame this story as a 'battle.' "[1]

This took place a few years before his ordination to the priesthood. Jim's involvement in these issues and his role as an interpreter of American Catholicism for the mass media would only grow.

As mentioned, he wrote in November 2000 an article titled, "The Church and the Homosexual Priest." He was attempting to answer, among others, Fr. Donald B. Cozzens, whose book, *The Changing Face of the Priesthood*, had been published earlier that year, spurring much debate. Jim made points he would make again and again for decades. Homosexually oriented priests are nothing new. There is no threat posed ipso facto by a homosexual priest. Being homosexual does not mean ipso facto that one is sexually active. The vow of celibacy functions the same for the homosexual priest as it does for the heterosexual one.[2]

He began to write and speak often about celibacy, as it was being called into question, as if trying to keep to such a vow was somehow the cause for the criminal behavior. In a 2002 op-ed in the *New York Times* he wrote, "[T]he value of celibacy is not the issue. It seems odd to have to point this out, but the vast majority—the overwhelming majority—of priests, sisters and brothers who take vows of celibacy keep their vows." Challengingly, he continued, "The unspoken question is: What kind of sick person would willingly give up sex? This is not a surprising reaction in a culture that prizes sex and sexuality and places such an emphasis on sexual expression."[3]

There is no reason to call into question the values, vows, and role of religious brothers, sisters, and priests, he was saying; it's simply criminal behavior that deserves the attention. Again, from the op-ed in the *Times*: "The criminal acts of a few do not negate the value of celibacy, any more than spousal abuse or incest can negate the value of marriage or marital love."

Nearly two decades later, he would tweet this when Catholic News Service broke a fresh story from Guam about an archbishop found guilty of abuse:

> The next step in the ongoing prevention of sexual abuse must be to hold bishops accountable who countenanced clergy sexual abuse, or moved around abusers, remove bishops found guilty of this, and then say explicitly that this is why they are being removed. It is the missing link.[4]

By then, he had also written in *The Jesuit Guide to (Almost) Everything*: "By the way, chastity doesn't lead to unhealthy behavior. The sex-abuse crisis in the Catholic Church was, as I see it, more about a small percentage of psychologically unhealthy men who should have never been admitted into seminaries or religious orders in the first place, and some bishops who should have never shuttled them from one parish to another, than it was about chastity per se."[5]

The only trouble with that comment, as it turned out, was that Jim spoke of the crisis in the past tense.

Consider his thoughtful attempt in the 2002 op-ed to explain the spiritual purposes of celibacy. He hoped to reveal to the large audience of thoughtful people reading the paper of record why an intelligent person might still take a vow that seems antiquated.

"Celibacy is . . . an ancient tradition of love," he wrote. "Celibacy is, in short, about loving others." That argument elicited cynicism from those already outraged by stories of priests molesting children in the sacristy. "Throughout the history of Christianity, celibacy has been part of a religious life dedicated to serving others," Jim also wrote. Again, that was difficult for Catholics to hear. The *Times* editors chose "Understanding love through asceticism" as the pull-quote for especially large type that day in the paper. What they might have better used was this:

> The pedophilia scandal is about sick priests, bishops who have made tragically wrong decisions about responding to criminal behavior and the silence of the Catholic Church on this matter.[6]

* * *

The Jesuit Guide to (Almost) Everything brought Jim's usual publisher some consternation. After the success of *My Life with the Saints* and his other extensive exposure in the media, Jim was in great demand. But while he expressed many times his gratitude and affection for the Jesuit-owned Loyola Press, when the deeper-pocketed publisher Harper-Collins asked Jim to write a general introduction to Jesuit spirituality, it was an offer that Jim didn't feel he should refuse. He told me recently how hard it was for him to leave Loyola Press after several years of working with them. But the notion of moving from a Catholic publisher to one potentially able to reach a broader nonreligious audience was appealing. Writing the books was, after all, all about reaching and ministering to people.

At the time, he asked the novelist Ron Hansen for advice. A long conversation weighed the pros and cons of staying with a smaller Catholic house versus going with a larger, mainstream firm. A few minutes into Jim's presentation, Ron said, simply, "No question. The bigger one."

His purpose in *The Jesuit Guide* was to introduce the riches of Ignatian spirituality for ordinary life to people seeking answers to everyday questions about meaning. As usual, he stated both his purpose and conclusions in language that is easily accessed by the nontheologically minded. Each of Jim's books is essentially spirituality for those who don't identify as too spiritual. For instance, in the chapter "What Do You Want?" he offers this conclusion:

> If God meets you where you are [he'd just explained how this might happen], then where you are is a place to meet God. You don't have to wait until your life settles down, or the kids move out of the house, or you've found that perfect apartment, or you recover from that long illness. You don't have to wait until you've overcome your sinful patterns, or you're more "religious" or you can pray "better."
> You don't have to wait for any of that.
> Because God is ready now.[7]

The book was published in early March 2010 and was on the bestseller lists within two months. *My Life with the Saints* had been Jim's first publishing "hit"—no question about that—but with the New York publisher's muscle, *The Jesuit Guide* would reach the *New York Times* list. It was a most unlikely topic for a bestseller. A book about St. Ignatius of Loyola and Jesuit spiritual practices? But what began as a work of mission created new opportunities for Ignatian spirituality to gain a hearing and an audience.

The strength and length of Jim's writing had been building over the years. After a relatively thin edited book, followed by writerly, friendly memoirs about working in the corporate world, becoming a Jesuit, and ministering in East Africa and Jamaica, *My Life with the Saints* had applied the same winsome approach to four hundred pages of saintly examples and principles for living. Then there were smaller books here and there until *The Jesuit Guide* took his audience further into serious reading on Ignatian spirituality. Jim must have realized that he could take them there. His writing always shows purpose, plan, and mission.

Very few at the time would have grasped this irony: As a novice in January 1989, the young Jim Martin was, for whatever reasons, deemed by his novice director not ready for his first-year thirty-day retreat with the Spiritual Exercises of St. Ignatius. Of the two *primi* that year, only one went to the retreat house at the appointed time that year. Jim had to wait until summer for his retreat and for his first immersion in the Exercises.

As that other *primi* recently said to me: "[Jim] may not have been ready, but he's made up for lost time!"[8]

* * *

His first appearance on *The Colbert Report* took place September 13, 2007. *The Colbert Report* was a satirical comedy variety and talk television show hosted by Stephen Colbert, known for his parodies of conservative politicians and opinions as a former correspondent of *The Daily Show with Jon Stewart*, which had a similar audience. On the program, Colbert famously remained in character as a narrow-minded, tunnel-vision conservative playing the host, parodying what he intended to critique. He would often interview progressive guests, asking questions presumably aimed at pointing out mistakes in their logic or assumptions, but the questions and opinions that were offered were exaggerated in such a way that the conservative agenda was, in the process, the one skewered.

Colbert's true personality and real-life views went unknown to his growing audience. He wrote bestselling books in the same voice and with the same opinions of his character as host of the show. He was even a guest on other television programs, still as the "Stephen Colbert" of *The Colbert Report*. Eventually, the world would learn that the real Colbert was a practicing Roman Catholic, but this would come out much later, after Fr. Jim had been named official "chaplain" of the show, an on-air job offer that viewers could tell caught Jim by surprise.

That first night on *The Colbert Report*, Jim was invited to talk about revelations in a recent book of correspondence to and from Mother Teresa that she'd spent decades living in spiritual darkness—"almost fifty years without sensing the presence of God in her life"—as read on-screen, quoting from the book, before Jim went on stage. "And judging from this photo," Colbert added, with a look and voice of faux sincerity, holding up *Time* magazine's cover story/photo, "that's like a third of her life."

One of Colbert's bookers had reached out to Jim after reading a piece he had published in the *New York Times* on August 29, which included this optimistic "take" on what many others—including the popular atheist Christopher Hitchens—were grabbing as evidence that Christian faith and optimism are unfounded. If a woman like Mother Teresa secretly admitted (the letters were never meant by her to be published) to disbelieving in God (she wrote of lacking belief for years at a time), then why should others believe? Jim had written in the *Times*: "Mother Teresa's ministry with the poor won her the Noble Prize and the admiration of a believing world. Her ministry to a doubting modern world may have just begun."

(Jim had had a similar conversation with Stephen Adly Guirgis two years earlier during his writing of his play. Everyone was fascinated with Mother Teresa's despair as the details of it slowly emerged after her death.)

"He was very kind to me in the green room," Jim remembers, speaking of Colbert that night, "and basically said what he always says, 'Treat me [my character] on the show like you would treat an idiot!' And that was the first time we met."

"*Saints* can have times when they don't believe in *God*?!" Colbert asked Jim halfway through the interview. And, "Why be good if you don't constantly feel the threat of heaven or hell?"

"I feel like I'm at my M.Div. comps now," responded Jim, laughing.

"I don't know what that means, but I assume I just nailed you," says Colbert.

"You *did* nail me," said Jim.

"Well, Father, it was a pleasure. Thank you so much for joining us." Then the segment abruptly ended.

Asked how he felt about that first appearance, Jim explained to me, "I felt like I had done a decent job, given that he was smiling and the audience was laughing. . . . I felt that . . . he treated me much better than he did many of his other guests." And, "At the time the show was at the height of its popularity and I was very happy most of all to be able to talk about something that meant a great deal to me—my faith—on a show like that. I knew that I'd reach more people in five minutes than in a year of homilies."[9]

About those dark nights of Mother Teresa, Jim would later say: "A person in darkness feels isolated from God. Yet with patience (whether or not one can identify which 'dark night' one is experiencing), one can let go of the need to feel God's presence constantly and gradually move through the darkness to discover greater intimacy with God."[10]

* * *

Since his school days, Jim had enjoyed a reputation for being witty, smart, and fun. Since becoming a Jesuit, he'd become interested in how humor—or its opposite—might build or divide the church. In this context, he wrote in 1997 about Sr. Wendy Beckett on television:

> Here is a woman religious who knows precisely what she's doing with a medium that many religious figures eschew. She stares frankly and directly at the camera, never condescends to the viewer and never apologizes for her frankly Christian outlook on life. She is honest, intelligent, serene and humorous. Just a few minutes of Sister Wendy on television, in fact, help counteract many seasons of negative stereotypes of priests, nuns and the like.[11]

He was conscious not only of negative stereotypes in the media about priests, religious, and the Catholic Church but also of priests and religious who present the faith more negatively than positively. Since 1995, for instance, he had criticized the negativity of Mother Angelica and the Eternal Word Television Network (EWTN). And he reflected: "Ever since Fulton Sheen went off the air, the Catholic Church has had a hard time harnessing the power of television."[12]

Some who knew Jim simply as a Jesuit who wrote for *America* had already marked him a liberal. He was conscious of this, writing hesitantly in that same television column ("I run the risk, I know, of getting into trouble if I write *anything* about Mother Angelica"):

> For some Americans she represents the Catholic Church. . . . Here, gentle readers, is a woman who loves her church and is devoted to God. It might not be the kind of church preferred by you St.-Louis-Jesuit-singing, Matthew-Fox-reading, inclusive-language, empower-the-laity types, but she's devoted to her church nonetheless.[13]

He spent a full page praising Mother Angelica and her network, followed by, "Now, for the second part of our story: Mother Angelica, devout and well-intentioned as she may be, has some big problems." By Jim's estimation, those problems were: "[she] seems to live in a world of black and white," ignoring nuance and complexity; "[she] seems to be . . . more comfortable with the past than with the present"; and "like many other American Catholics, Mother Angelica is angry." Each accusation was well-argued but sure to infuriate the "right" against Jim's "left." He concluded: "The Catholic Church, as projected by Mother Angelica, is one, holy, catholic and apostolic. It is also extremely angry. And this particular fruit of her television ministry is a signal disservice to the American church."

The battle with Mother Angelica only increased over time. Jim seems to have felt that the vision of Catholicism she portrayed was the antithesis of his own life and ministry as a Catholic in active ministry.

There was, for instance, the time in early 1998 when Cardinal Roger Mahony of Los Angeles issued a pastoral letter on the Eucharist to the members of his archdiocese that Mother Angelica took issue with, denouncing it on EWTN for not emphasizing enough the doctrine of transubstantiation. She said to the camera: "I'm afraid my obedience in that diocese would be absolutely zero. And I hope that everyone else's would be zero, too."

Martin quotes this, and adds, "Lest anyone miss the point, she held up her hand and brought her forefinger and thumb together to form a big zero." The cardinal didn't ignore Mother Angelica's protest. He demanded an apology, and when one wasn't forthcoming, he threatened to bring a case against her to the Congregation for the Institutes of Consecrated Life at the Vatican, invoking two articles of canon law. One is about respecting the teaching of bishops. The other speaks most directly to the point:

> [a] person who publicly incites his or her subjects to hatred or animosity against the Apostolic See or the Ordinary because of some act of ecclesiastical authority or ministry, or who provokes . . . to disobedience against them, is to be published by interdict or other just penalties. (Can. 1373)

The cardinal would have a good case. Jim took his case to his audience in *America*. "What is an American Catholic to make of all of this?" he asked.

* * *

It was nearly a decade after taking on Mother Angelica's angry approach that Jim became interested in turning to more serious study of a topic that had engaged him his full life: humor. The University of Pennsylvania self-described "lukewarm" Catholic telling jokes at the expense of Catholic foibles had become the Jesuit priest studying joy and laughter in the gospels and the saints. It seems to have begun—as usual—with a feature in a 2007 issue of *America*: "The Most Infallible Sign: Recovering Joy, Humor and Laughter in the Spiritual Life." He quoted saints who laughed, defended lightheartedness as close to godliness, and found humor and humanity in the life of Jesus.

Four years later, this would turn into a book, *Between Heaven and Mirth*, with a similar subtitle: *Why Joy, Humor and Laughter Are at the Heart of the Spiritual Life*. This one even featured an endorsement from Stephen Colbert: "Jim is a Jesuit priest and a funny guy. I'm grateful to know both of him." One detects a writer's skill developing over those years, as Jim's style became even more accessible to ordinary readers. For example, what was "The undervaluing of Christian humor is particularly surprising in light of Gospel stories in which Jesus evinces playfulness" becomes, in the book, "What I see as the undervaluing of humor in church circles is even more surprising when we look carefully at the person of Jesus, whom the Gospels reveal as a man with a palpable sense of joy and even playfulness."[14]

He'd realized, while giving hundreds of talks for *My Life with the Saints* just how important humor and laughter were to the saints he loved. Likewise, while giving those talks he saw how surprised audiences were not only to hear stories about the humor of the saints but also to consider the possibility that Jesus had a sense of humor. And working with Stephen Adly Guirgis off Broadway, who was free with his language and outlook in order to help people understand the gospels, gave Jim more freedom to be irreverent.

He demonstrates in *Between Heaven and Mirth* how humor can be a way of humility, knowing, and evangelism. By this time, Jim was a fixture on the lecture circuit in large Catholic parishes, retreat centers, and universities—with humor as his topic. One such talk Jim gave at St. Mary of the Nativity Church in Scituate, near Boston, was summarized by a reporter for the *Patriot Ledger*. The newspaper listed with bullet points ten reasons, according to Jim, why Christians need to laugh:

- Humor and joy are a way to evangelize. "They show you have faith in God, and are living your own vocation joyfully."

- Humor is a tool for humility. "It helps deflate the ego."

- Humor shocks listeners into recognizing reality. "It speaks truth to power."

- Humor can express Christian courage.

- It deepens our relationship with God. "Can you allow God to be playful with you?"

- Humor welcomes others.

- It's healing.

- It fosters good relations in our work.

- Humor opens our minds.

- And it's just plain fun. "A foretaste of heaven."[15]

He also began to use humor more often to deflect his own growing fame, observing the second of those bullet points. There was the time, for instance, when he was invited to participate on a panel of scholars at a meeting of the Catholic Theological Society of America, which was meeting that year in San Jose, California. Joining Lawrence S. Cunningham, emeritus professor at Notre Dame, and Wendy M. Wright, professor of theology at Creighton University, to talk about "Scripting the Saints," Jim quipped:

> A few weeks ago, I was at a party populated mainly by young Catholic theologians. It was an enjoyable evening in celebration of a friend's having received tenure at a certain Jesuit university located in New York. So I was telling one theologian about [this] upcoming CTSA panel.
>
> "You know," I said, "I was thinking of starting off light-heartedly, by telling the scholars that I might be the only one in the room without a Ph.D."
>
> "Oh, don't worry," she deadpanned, "They'll know already."[16]

There were, however, other moments when he told a joke that perhaps went too far. Jim is a believer in practicing careful discernment in such matters. "You have to ask yourself, would it needlessly offend someone? How would I feel about myself after I've said it?" he once explained to me in response to the question, "How do you know if it is okay to tell a particular joke?"

But then he remembered that there was the time when he told a joke about a Jesuit, Franciscan, and Dominican on Krista Tippett's public radio show *On Being*—only to later regret having told it at all. Jim emailed and asked the producer if she could take it out of the broadcast segment. So now the interview is online as edited.[17]

CHAPTER SEVEN

A Life with Jesus

Thomas Merton was the one who pointed Jim Martin to religious and spiritual life while Jim was still in the corporate world, but Jesus was the one Jim principally turned toward and related to. Jesus is the focus of the Ignatian Spiritual Exercises, which Jim first experienced in the novitiate. A desire to contemplate, understand, and be present with Jesus fills the letters he wrote home to family and friends at that time and the first articles he wrote for publication.

In late 1993, Jim published "Frustrations—Jesus' Ministry and Ours," from Nairobi, an article primarily for other members of religious orders. Making apologies that he was not a real Scripture scholar, he said: "I have come to the . . . conclusion that as a flesh-and-blood human being Jesus must have felt frustrated." Then he speaks of his own difficulties in East Africa. "The anger and frustration that I feel for the refugees whom I know is inescapable. The more I reflect on it, the less I feel guilty about it. Jesus got angry. And so do I. What other response can one expect?"[1]

Thousands of hours spent in Ignatian meditation taught Jim about Jesus. Then, several pilgrimages to the places of the Holy Land opened his eyes to the facts of the Jesus of history and the Christ of faith, who in Jim's experience were one and the same. His theology studies with Daniel J. Harrington, SJ, among others, sparked a love for learning about Jesus' milieu in the first-century Roman Empire and nascent Rabbinic Judaism. He had also demonstrated his passion for Jesus studies when he put the scholarship of Harrington, Elizabeth Johnson, John Meier, and Raymond Brown to popular use on the off-Broadway set of *The Last Days of Judas Iscariot.*

So twenty-some years after that essay from Nairobi it wasn't surprising to anyone who knew him that Jim was planning a book about Jesus. What surprised them was how big the book would become. It was almost twice the length of the sizable *My Life with the Saints.*

At a time when the other most recognized Catholic priest in America, Father Robert Barron (a frequent contributor to the culture section of *America* while Jim was culture editor), was writing and filming his multipart video series, *Catholicism,* explaining the faith with attention to works of art, saints, traditions, and theological fine points (the first two episodes released on June 1, 2014), Jim was returning to a subject that unites all Christians, perhaps all people: Jesus. His book would be fueled by extensive scholarly research, firsthand experience in the places of Jesus' earthly existence, but also a rich Ignatian imaginative life. As one practiced in the Exercises, Jim knew what it was like to place oneself in a gospel scene and to imagine "walking" with Jesus, "talking with," and "listening to" Jesus.

"How do you avoid your imagination becoming cinematic, as in imagining a Robert Powell [the actor from *Jesus of Nazareth*, the 1977 blockbuster directed by Franco Zeffirelli] Jesus, instead of an image of Jesus that might be brought to you by the Holy Spirit?" I once asked Jim. He replied:

> Part of it is being okay with whatever images you have in your head, like Robert Powell, and knowing that God can work even through a cinematic image. It's almost impossible for me to picture Jesus's face anyway, a grace I've never been given, so I tend to focus more on him as a kind of "whole person." That is, someone walking beside me, or ahead of me, or speaking to me. I've never looked him in the eye, and he's never looked me in the eye. Yet.

"How does one practice Ignatian imagination without becoming caught up in one's personal drama? How does one guard against that?"

> Sometimes it's okay to get caught up in your own "drama," providing that is what God is asking you to look at. But it's actually easy to enter into a Gospel scene even when there is a lot of turmoil or drama in your life. In fact, it's often a relief. What a joy to be with Jesus in Capernaum when things are tough in your life, or in Jerusalem when you are facing problems, or on the way to Caesarea Philippi with the disciples when you're worried. But at some point in the meditation your own drama may indeed come up. A good spiritual director, or more experience in prayer, will help you discern when it's a distraction and when it's something God is asking you to look at. It's an important question in prayer.[2]

It was from this firsthand experience (unusual, to be sure, among those who turn to scholarship on Jesus) that Jim sought to go, not deeper, but more broadly into the sources, texts, and discoveries of the historical Jesus who is also the Jesus that a Christian encounters in faith.

Other experience came in the form of personal pilgrimage to the places where Jesus walked. The first of these trips, in 2011, he made with George Williams, a Jesuit friend who had entered the novitiate one year ahead of him. George, who had for years worked as a prison chaplain (and was then Catholic chaplain at San Quentin Prison in California) was one of Jim's closest friends. Shortly after Jim had decided to travel to the Holy Land, he discovered that George was not only free during those weeks but also interested in coming along. Their travels together—with George offering droll comments about the pilgrimage throughout—helped to make Jim's book on Jesus not only educational and inspirational but enjoyable.

But even with his lighthearted friend along, the trip was a profound, and deeply serious, experience for Jim. One night he wrote in his journal:

Aug. 26
Another amazing day. Seeing the Sea of Galilee was a highlight of my life. . . .

Finally I saw a glimpse of the Sea of Galilee and was startled by how beautiful it was and how I recognized the landscape, especially the folds of the mountains. And as we got closer to the Mount of Beatitudes it grew more beautiful. Pinkish-grey hills and a lovely blue green sea, a cornflower blue. Lovely.

This afternoon we dropped off our stuff and looked around and went to Tabgha, where the miracle of the Feeding of the 5,000 happened. We prayed in the quiet chapel, and I felt a strange feeling when I realized I was right where not just any miracle occurred, like in Lourdes or elsewhere, but a miracle of Jesus. It put all the other miracles in their place. Just so foundational and life changing for me. Profound.

When I got back to the monastery, a little overwhelmed, I opened to the passage where Jesus said, "Follow me," and I cried. Looking out over the Sea of Galilee, I could almost hear him say it to them, and to me. He said it here! I can't describe what I felt other than it sounded real and grounded and new. Then at one point I was looking at my guide book and saw the back cover and noticed a photo of a red-domed church on the Sea of Galilee. It was Capernaum. And I looked out my window and saw it. I can see Jesus's town, where he spent many months, from my window! Amazing. I have always wanted to see this.

Today I feel as if I have seen something of what heaven is like. I wanted to just look at the Sea.

Tonight the hills were pink and lovely. Jesus saw this.

* * *

To read the lengthy acknowledgments (not to mention the almost thirty pages of endnotes) in *Jesus: A Pilgrimage*, published in March 2014, is to realize what a vast undertaking this project was. The book is dedicated to Daniel J. Harrington, SJ, Jim's old professor from Weston, who died only a few weeks before the book released. Harrington was a friend, mentor, and teacher to Jim, and he had reviewed and critiqued the complete manuscript. "I believe him to have been a saint," Jim wrote in *America* the day after Harrington's death, adding: "Today I feel like I see the Gospels through Dan's eyes. That may sound odd, but what I mean is that I see the Gospels with both the eyes of faith and a critical mind. Dan's approach was sensible, moderate, scholarly, curious, just, balanced, cautious, generous but, above all, faithful."[3] Other scholars are thanked in the acknowledgments, including Amy-Jill Levine, a chaired professor in New Testament at Vanderbilt and Jewish expert on the early church.

From his publisher's perspective, the riskiest thing about *Jesus* was its 550 densely typeset pages. Would Jim's audience be willing to take on such a read?

They were. This too became a *New York Times* bestseller. The reader was able to feel that they were there in the Holy Land, walking from Bethlehem to Nazareth to the Jordan River to Jerusalem to the Sea of Galilee, with an author who was also a fellow seeker, pondering answers to questions raised by the gospel accounts. Jim wrote with his usual humor, wit, and insight, introducing theology, biblical commentary, and historical studies gently, always through the lens of his own faith. That remains the most unusual aspect of this priest's writings: his willingness to view principles of faith (the usual domain of priestly writing and lecturing) through the subjectivity of his own experience (much less common).

By chapter 22 of this pilgrimage, the reader finds himself standing in the Church of the Holy Sepulchre in Jerusalem. Chapter 22 is all about the risen Christ, and, as usual, Jim shows that this is not a book of disinterested scholarship. "The Resurrection is the center of my faith," he writes, and, "Every day I return to that theme—or more broadly, the story of the death and resurrection of Jesus." He writes inspiringly about the hope and joy of the resurrection and what it means for everyday life. Speaking again personally, he writes:

> Often I return to the image of the terrified disciples cowering behind closed doors. We are not called to live in that room. We are called to emerge from our hiding places and to accompany Mary, weeping sometimes, searching always,

and ultimately blinded by the dawn of Jesus's new life—
surprised—delighted and moved to joy. We are called to
believe what she has seen: he is risen.[4]

Jim's book would involve still more people in the life of
Christ in another, unexpected, way, beyond its impact on
hundreds of thousands of readers. Shortly after the book's
publication, the new, young, editor in chief of *America*, Matt
Malone, SJ, asked Jim if he would be interested in leading
pilgrimages to the Holy Land. Father Malone sensed there
would be an interest based on the enormous sales of *Jesus:
A Pilgrimage*. Jim initially demurred but eventually agreed.
The pilgrimages became annual events, attracting as many
as one hundred pilgrims a year from across the world, with
hundreds more on the waiting list, eager to visit Galilee and
Judea and experience the Jesus of history and the Christ of
faith.

The great irony was that, as Jim confesses in *Jesus*, he
initially balked at going to the Holy Land at all. Malone's
predecessor, Drew Christiansen, SJ, had urged Jim to visit
during the research for his upcoming book. As he admits in
Jesus, he was concerned that his own mental images of sites
that he had prayed about for years would be sullied by
"locales overrun with tourists."

So the Jesuit who initially had no intention of ever visiting the Holy Land added another ministry to his already
full life: pilgrim leader.

* * *

While Jim was in the final stages of writing *Jesus: A Pilgrimage*, the first Jesuit in history was elected as supreme pontiff,
and that pope became enormously popular—a media star.

So it was a busy time. *Time* magazine called in March 2013, inviting Jim to write for a Time Inc. Specials newsstand book/magazine on Pope Francis to be issued quickly. Jim sent them "The Life of a Jesuit," which *Time*'s editors subtitled "A Noted Author on Why He Loves Being a Priest."

Jim used the opening paragraphs to summarize his own journey to the priesthood, mentioning his "loving Catholic family, but not one that was super-religious," studying at Wharton, six years at General Electric, happening upon the Merton documentary on television, and his ordination in June 1999 at St. Ignatius of Loyola Church in Chestnut Hill, Massachusetts. Then he took his time explaining the basics of what priests do, where they work, what promises they make. One of those promises is, of course, celibacy, and Jim offered an opinion that he'd stated many times before but rarely to such a large audience:

> Celibacy doesn't lead to sexual abuse, but that doesn't mean commentators don't draw that conclusion. Most incidents of abuse take place in the family, but no one says marriage leads to sexual abuse. Many incidents take place in schools, but no one says a degree in education leads to abusing children. Basically, the easy (and insulting) conflation of celibacy with pedophilia reflects a discomfort with the celibate life. Anyone who chooses to live without sexual intimacy, the popular thinking goes, must be either sick, deluded, crazy—or all three.[5]

He concluded by summarizing what he loves most about being a priest: hearing confessions and offering words of forgiveness, celebrating the Mass, and baptizing people into the faith. "I wish more people felt called to the priesthood," he writes, with a sense that perhaps the new pontiff will inspire some more. *Time* sent a photographer to meet Jim at the Church of St. Ignatius Loyola in New York City, still his local parish, to take a lush full-page photograph that appeared on page twenty-nine of the priest in his vestments holding a missal.

Meanwhile, there were opportunities for *America*, as a Jesuit weekly, to be a more prominent religious voice in the United States with the advent of the first Jesuit pope. Jim had the idea of the magazine doing an exclusive interview with Pope Francis. He suggested it to his boss, Matt Malone, SJ, in late April, about six weeks into Francis's papacy. This would prove a coup of large proportions, resulting in a full issue devoted to the exclusive on September 30, 2013, followed quickly by a book, *A Big Heart Open to God*, issued by Jim's publisher, HarperOne, which included spiritual reflections by Jim as well.[6]

There would be much more of this kind of writing. Two years later, Jim accepted an invitation to write a piece titled "Francis, Superstar" for *Philadelphia* magazine in anticipation of the papal trip to that city. The magazine's contents page summarized it: "Fellow Jesuit (and native Philadelphian) James Martin sizes up the rock-star pope's appeal."[7] For a brief time, the Catholic Church, the Society of Jesus, and the papacy rode a wave of popularity.

* * *

This was also a time when Jim returned to the theater—becoming a consultant to the great director Martin Scorsese in his long-awaited adaptation of Shūsaku Endō's *Silence*, a novel about Jesuit missionary martyrs in seventeenth-century Japan.

As we've seen, Jim hadn't always reviewed directors, actors, and films with religious themes generously. Years earlier,

Jim wrote about Scorsese in the context of reviewing films about Jesus that a Catholic might want to rent on videotape. He discussed the controversial *The Last Temptation of Christ* (1988), revealing that he'd seen the film in the theater and remembered being "accosted by five women brandishing rosary beads and telling me where I would end up at the end of my earthly life." Mother Angelica went to great lengths to publicly condemn the film on EWTN, he added, but he found it worthwhile. Praising the research the director and his team had conducted, the then-young Jesuit wrote:

> All of this distracted from an innovative film about the life of Christ. . . . Admittedly, Willem Dafoe makes for a strange Jesus. . . . But it is an evocative look at the time and the man and well worth a $3.50 rental at Blockbuster.[8]

Such comments were not what led Scorsese's team to seek out Jim as a consultant. Nearly twenty years later, and after his experience with Stephen Adly Giurgis, Philip Seymour Hoffman, Sam Rockwell, and John Patrick Shanley, Jim had grown in his understanding of film and theater. In those early reviews for *America* he had focused only on the "outside" of a film: its effects on viewers. He now once again had the opportunity to be involved very much on the "inside."

The specific passion that led to *Jesus: A Pilgrimage* also guided Jim in his work on the film with Scorsese and his team. As Jim recently explained to me:

> For many years, I felt strange about what I considered almost an obsession with Jesus. I read anything about the Gospels that I could find, about the historical Jesus, about daily life in first-century Judea and Galilee, about how the Gospels were written and so on. I could never get enough of it. And when I took my first New Testament class with

Dan Harrington, I felt like I didn't want to study anything else. I had the same experience during my philosophy studies when I studied New Testament Greek. I couldn't believe how much I enjoyed reading the Gospels in their original language. Eventually, I realized this fascination with Jesus was one way that God had of drawing me to Jesus. Then I just sort of accepted it.

So when I was helping Martin Scorsese with *Silence*, there was a scene in one of the early scripts that didn't quite ring true. The main character, a Jesuit priest, was talking about his love for Jesus, and it seemed a little flat. I suggested the word that seemed to sum up my own relationship: *fascinated*. And that's what ended up in the final script. Jesus fascinates me. I love reading about him, thinking about him, and praying to him. One day, I hope, I'll meet him face to face.[9]

Silence starred Andrew Garfield and Adam Driver as young missionaries who in the seventeenth century travel to Japan seeking their mentor, a middle-aged priest, played by Liam Neeson, who is rumored to have apostatized. It released worldwide three days before Christmas in 2016. Jim's involvement in the project began two years before release, reviewing the script, working with Scorsese's historical consultant and making suggestions to improve the authenticity of how the Jesuit priests would behave and respond to situations. As he explained:

At one point in the final script [Garfield's character] quotes directly from the Exercises, and I remember saying, "This is what he would say in this situation." They were open to that. For instance, a quote that comes directly from the Exercises, that to me is very powerful to see in the movie: "What have I done for Christ? What am I doing for Christ? What ought I do for Christ?" is there.[10]

His work on *Silence* also went beyond the script to advising the actors. He and Garfield worked closely on the Jesuit mind-set. Garfield was then directed for several months through the complete Spiritual Exercises by Jim. In the same way that his consulting for Stephen Guirgis and Sam Rockwell had become more involved, this project too took on a bigger than anticipated scope. Soon, Jim developed a friendship with Martin Scorsese, as well, and became a spiritual adviser to Garfield as well as his spiritual director—relationships that continue to this day.

For Garfield, the experience was life-changing. In an interview in *America* with a young Jesuit after the film's release, he spoke of the experience of being directed through the Exercises:

> "What was really easy was falling in love with this person, was falling in love with Jesus Christ. That was the most surprising thing."
>
> He fell silent at the thought of it, clearly moved to emotion. He clutched his chest, just below the sternum, somewhere between his gut and his heart, and what he said next came out through bursts of laughter: "God! That was the most remarkable thing—falling in love, and how easy it was to fall in love with Jesus."[11]

* * *

The range of Jim's involvement in all his ventures, throughout 2014 and 2015, is astounding by any standard. He was also preparing a book based on homilies he gave at St. Patrick's Cathedral in New York City on Good Friday 2015 at this time.

Seven Last Words was released on February 2, 2016, and was designed to be an accessible and practical application of what Jim had written in *Jesus: A Pilgrimage*—an invitation to the reader to discover or deepen a real friendship with Jesus.

Each of the seven sayings of Jesus as he hung on the cross—"Father, forgive them, for they do not know what they do"; "Today you will be with me in Paradise"; "Woman, this is your son . . . This is your mother"; etc.— is offered with Ignatian exercises and understanding for experiencing and listening to Jesus in those moments.

Jim was intent, in each of the meditations, to demonstrate that Good Friday (the day on which these seven last words were said by Christ) is not meant to define a Christian life. As he wrote in his conclusion: "Jesus's public ministry was largely a ministry of joy, not suffering. Encountering him meant encountering the joy that characterizes the reign of God. So we should not reduce his life simply to that of the 'Suffering Servant,' as important as that image is in the Gospels."[12]

And he was also writing a novel.

The Abbey had a strange beginning. "I had an incredibly vivid dream, which began with a baseball shattering a window in my neighbor's home, and included not only the names of the characters, but the abbey itself: St. Philip and James. It was quite remarkable. Not long after two unusual things happened: I was visiting the Trappist monastery upon which I based the book and had a long conversation about the novel. Several days later I realized I had visited on the Feast of Philip and James. The unconscious is not only powerful but creative," Jim has said.[13]

Long before he contemplated writing a novel, Jim had a gifted ear for dialogue. This is just one rather randomly selected evidence of this, taken from *A Jesuit Off-Broadway*:

I had been following the news of the casting as Stephen
[Adly Giurgis] labored over selecting the right actors. . . .

"They're looking for Jesus now," I told a Jesuit friend.
He laughed. "Who isn't?"[14]

By the time Jim wrote *The Abbey*, he also had famous
novelist friends—Ron Hansen, for instance. The two met
when Jim was compiling his first book, *How Can I Find
God?* Jim had reached out, on a lark, to John Irving, asking
the author of *A Prayer for Owen Meany* if he would contribute. Irving demurred but referred Jim to his friend and
former student at the University of Iowa's Writers Work-
shop, Hansen, who then gladly wrote something for the
book. Their next professional connection came when Jim
asked Hansen to write a foreword to his memoir, *This Our
Exile*. Hansen gladly did so, but then Jim's publisher at
Orbis decided to ask Robert Coles instead; Hansen's was
never used.

Over the years, Jim had recommended Hansen's novel
Mariette in Ecstasy, about the religious experiences of a
young nun, to dozens of audiences and in print on many
occasions. "He's been a great champion of my fiction,"
Hansen told me, "so he was somewhat tentative about getting my reactions to his own try at the form. Jim said in an
interview that he would have liked me to edit and rewrite
it, but *The Abbey* was so *him* that I was reluctant to make
it in even the slightest way mine. I commented that it was
'A sheer delight—funny, engaging, deep, and moving.' Like
Jim. That praise was my sole contribution to his fine novel."[15]

Another literary star who endorsed the novel was poet
and bestselling memoirist, Mary Karr. Jim had met her a
few years earlier in New York City at a fundraising benefit
for Busted Halo, the media company and radio show run

by the Paulist Fathers. Karr and Martin were both there as invited speakers. They had priest friends in common who were also present: Fr. Edward Beck, CP, then cohost of *Focus on Faith* with Chris Cuomo on ABC News; and Fr. Dave Dwyer, the Paulist priest who was the face and voice behind Busted Halo. Karr mentioned to Jim that she was seeking somewhere in the city where she might do the Spiritual Exercises with an experienced director. Initially he demurred, since he already had a full schedule of directees.

A few months later, Jim emailed her to say that he had an opening in his schedule for spiritual direction; was she interested? She was. Karr has seen Jim as spiritual director ever since. She says that he has given her a stronger practice of the Daily Examen, the Jesuit prayer that invites people to find God in their everyday life.

Specifically, "He's helped me to see how many small spiritual experiences I have of Jesus all the time." This has been a focus of Jim's ministry, not only in spiritual direction, for many years. He also wrote at about this time: "[O]ur search for God is often like Naaman's [see 2 Kgs 5]. We're searching for something spectacular to convince us of God's presence. Yet it is in the simple things, common events and common longings, where God may be found."[16]

As for the endorsement of *The Abbey*, Mary Karr says that Jim never asked her for it. His publisher also never asked. She insisted, and had to keep insisting, to see the manuscript and then to write what publishers call a "blurb" for the back cover.

"He was like the cat with the claws around the door," Karr says, so protective was Jim of not mixing up a spiritual directee with his writing career.[17]

CHAPTER EIGHT

Reaching Out to the Margins

I try to consciously stay away from anything that's overly political, because that's outside of my wheelhouse, and also I think it's not a good thing for priests or religious to get involved in that way. But as we see from Pope Francis, if I tweet something out that is something from the Gospel, or is based on what Jesus taught, and it has political implications, that doesn't bother me.

—James Martin, SJ[1]

The *Building a Bridge* episode in Jim's life might appear to contradict the statement that heads this chapter, but not to Jim's understanding.

His most controversial and most publicized book by tenfold, *Building a Bridge: How the Catholic Church and the LGBT Community Can Enter into a Relationship of Respect, Compassion, and Sensitivity*, first appeared in June 2017. Its subject and message were incredibly simple: the Catholic Church should show greater respect to one of its significant constituencies, LGBT people, and, correspondingly, the LGBT community should be more willing to listen and show respect to the teaching and institutions of the church to which they belong. That's not politics.

Jim saw the need for the book in the immediate aftermath of the Pulse nightclub shooting in Orlando, Florida, on June 12, 2016. A gunman opened fire in a nightclub known to be a popular gay hangout, killing forty-nine people, wounding fifty-three. Stories swirled in the media beginning the following day as to the shooter's sexual orientation and to occasions when the shooter had expressed hatred toward gay people. Jim noticed that only a handful of Catholic bishops spoke publicly to condemn the mass shooting, and most of those who *did* speak about the tragedy did not acknowledge or express condolences to the LGBT community or gay people. Jim posted a video to his public Facebook page on the subject that immediately went viral, garnering almost two million views in a few days.

Only a few weeks later, he was invited by New Ways Ministry, a group that ministers to and advocates for LGBT Catholics, to receive its Building Bridges Award. Knowing this might prove controversial, he sought and received permission from his own provincial in New York, the provincial of the Maryland Province (the talk would be in Baltimore), and the editor in chief of *America*. The talk was widely discussed and appeared on *America*'s website.

Naturally, his publisher asked if he might turn the talk into a book. He agreed. In addition to expanding the initial talk, he added what he has called "the more important part of the book," Bible passages and reflection questions to help people pray about the marginalization of LGBT people in the church.

Beyond that, Jim also sought, as he had for all of his books, the *imprimi potest* from his provincial, formal ecclesiastical approval to publish. Even though nothing in the book challenges church teaching, he wanted the support of his religious order, perhaps anticipating the blowback. In addition, he received endorsements from some of the most powerful and influential leaders in the church, including, crucially, Cardinal Kevin Farrell, the prefect of the Vatican's Dicastery for Laity, Family and Life. Still, even with the Jesuits' approval and the long list of cardinals and bishops endorsing the book, the book took some guts to write.

He attributes some of the courage to write it, knowing it would be controversial, to hearing a word from Jesus in a moment of prayer: "Must everyone like you?" It was a transforming moment for Jim.

The setting was his annual eight-day retreat at the Linwood Spiritual Center in Rhinebeck, New York, a few years before his public LGBT ministry began. Jim had always struggled with the desire to be liked, and he found it hard, as most people do, when he knew he wasn't liked. At the time when he heard the word from Jesus in prayer, there was someone in his Jesuit community who despised him, even to the point of refusing to speak to him. Jim was on retreat and praying over the story of the rejection at Nazareth from the Gospel of Luke, chapter 4.

Typically, that gospel passage about Jesus proclaiming who he is, and the people of his hometown rejecting him, is interpreted by many homilists as follows: we often don't see God right in front of us. But that day on retreat Jim realized something different: Jesus knew all those people. Jim knew from his research that Nazareth in Jesus' time was a small town of only two hundred to four hundred people, and they all knew him. Jesus would have had a good idea how they would respond when he proclaimed himself Messiah. Jim remembers:

So in prayer I asked Jesus, "How were you able to do this?"
How were you able to put up with the rejection?" I really
wanted to know how Jesus dealt with the contempt. And
in prayer, I heard Jesus say to me: "Must everyone like
you?" It was one of the few times that I've heard (not
physically, but rather they came into my head) such a clear
statement in prayer. And of course, at that point in my life,
I would have said, "Yes!"

He has returned to that memory and experience many times.
With the publication of *Building a Bridge*, this became an
important touch point.

"I've seen that as an invitation to move away from the
need for everyone to love you, like you or even approve of
you. That's enabled me to do the LGBT ministry with a
much freer heart," he explained to me.[2]

The initial response to the book could fairly be described
as adulation. In the first few days and weeks after its publication, Jim spoke at parishes and colleges and was often
met not only with full houses and standing ovations but
with grateful LGBT people (and their parents and grand-
parents) who waited in line to have their books signed and
to hug him and tell him, often tearfully, how grateful they
were for the book.

Father John Unni, the charismatic pastor of St. Cecilia
Church in the Back Bay section of Boston, invited Jim to
speak a few weeks after the book's initial publication. (There
would eventually be a second, longer, paperback edition of
the book.) Jim had spoken about Jesus at St. Cecilia's just a
few months before, and he told me that, given his recent appearance, the fact that the parish already had a thriving LGBT
outreach program, and the timing of the event—a weekday
night—he expected a sparse crowd.

Instead, seven hundred people packed the church, applauded for some several minutes, and then dozens stood in line for two hours to greet him. He was stunned by the reaction.

The next stage, which followed quickly, came when the book was discovered by some far-right Catholic websites and magazines. They didn't agree at all for the need for a "bridge," to put it mildly. Websites carried articles and videos vigorously (and often viciously) condemning the book.

But beyond simple disapproval, those who disagree with Jim's message seem at times to despise him personally. "I am Catholic and anti-Christian," said Benito Mussolini, which is how some in the church seem to behave with campaigns against Jim's message of love and acceptance. They will have none of it and seek to silence him with a variety of means, including innuendo, letter writing, calling campaigns to bishops' offices, and protests when Jim is invited to a diocese, school, or parish to speak. "Homosexualist Jesuit Fr. James Martin is a facile, worm-tongued deceiver and false teacher," began one commentary on a Catholic website with a large following.[3] It also has become common for Jim to encounter not only occasional protests but a handful of menacing questioners after a talk, pointing fingers in his face, accusing him of heresy.

"The Scariest Catholic in America," read the tongue-in-cheek headline of an early February 2018 op-ed in the Sunday *New York Times*. The sympathetic article about Jim by author Frank Bruni chronicled several cancelled speaking events around the United States and in London, all of which were to have been talks about Jesus, not LGBT acceptance, adding:

> Check out the websites and Twitter accounts of far-right Catholic groups and you'll see why. To them Father Martin

is "sick," "wicked," "a filthy liar," "the smoke of Satan" and a "heretic" on a fast track to "eternal damnation." They obsessively stalk him and passionately exhort churchgoers to protest his public appearances or prevent them from happening altogether.[4]

Before a talk at Sacred Heart University in early 2019, for example, Jim arrived to see lines of protesters, after weeks of online complaints and writing campaigns from conservatives who accused the Connecticut school's president of betraying Catholic values by inviting Jim to speak. Jim, as usual, seemed unfazed.

He concluded his talk that evening by telling the gospel story of Jesus entering Jericho and calling to Zacchaeus, the chief tax collector, who, wanting desperately to see Jesus, was hiding in a tree. Tax collectors were colluders with Rome and therefore viewed as grievous sinners. Jim asked his audience to see Zacchaeus as an image of the LGBT person today—"not because LGBT people are any more sinful than anyone else, because we're all sinners, but because he's the most marginalized person in town."

Jesus, surrounded by his followers, calls out to Zacchaeus and tells him he wants to stay at his house—*his* house, rather than any other. Jim said, "And this is my favorite line in the whole Gospel story," and then quoted, "And all who saw it began to grumble" (Luke 19:7).

Who are those grumbling?—Jim then asked. Answer: the followers of Jesus, the crowd closest to him, who he then explained are like the protesters outside or the hateful crowd online. "Extending mercy to those who are seen as 'other' makes people angry."

Then, Jim concluded: "It seems to me that there are two places to stand. You can stand with the crowd who grumbles and who opposes an offer of mercy to people on the margins. Or you can stand with Zacchaeus, or more importantly, you can stand with Jesus."

* * *

While writing *Building a Bridge*, Jim consulted with theologian James Alison and read his book *Faith Beyond Resentment*. Alison was one of the first gay priests in the Catholic Church to be open about his sexuality. *Faith Beyond Resentment*, subtitled *Fragments Catholic and Gay*, was published sixteen years before Jim's book—which leads to the obvious question, why was Jim's message such a shock to the Catholic system? Why the intense reaction on both sides: those who were grateful to Jim and those who wanted to see him kicked out of the priesthood? Much of the ground had been previously covered. Answers take various forms.

First, Jim is a priest with a broad national and international audience, while Alison is read mostly by other theologians. Jim is also a priest with a pastoral focus, not with a parish, but with many pastoral ministries. Alison is rarely seen and rarely functions in his priestly role. And Jim is the author of bestsellers, while Alison's books sell in the hundreds. Jim wrote and taught on popular, foundational subjects such as Jesus and Ignatian spirituality, while Alison writes on controversial topics such as this one.

Most subtle of all is the fact that Jim is a cradle Catholic, while Alison converted from Anglicanism. And Jim writes as a priest with a heart for mission and evangelization, while Alison writes mainly as a gay man reflecting on how the church has hurt him.

A healthier, more compassionate understanding of sexuality in the church was Jim's hope with *Building a Bridge*. But the Catholic Church is still in the heat and humiliation of ongoing clergy sex-abuse scandals. There has been wave after wave.

For instance, when it became public that the retired, influential Cardinal Theodore McCarrick of Washington, DC, had hidden sexual relationships with, and harassment of, seminarians for decades, James Alison wrote two features for *The Tablet* in London. In the first, he showed another reason why his writing hadn't done years earlier what Jim's was quickly accomplishing now:

> [A] few years ago I found myself leading a retreat for Italian gay priests in Rome. Of the nearly 50 participants some were single, some partnered, for others it was the first time they could talk honestly with other priests outside the confessional. Among them there were seven or eight mid-level Vatican officials. I asked one from the Congregation for the Clergy what he made of those attending with their partners. He smiled and said, "Of course, we know that the partnered ones are the healthy ones." Let that sink in. In the clerical closet, dishonesty is functional, honesty is dysfunctional, and the absence or presence of circumspect sexual practice between adult males is irrelevant.[5]

Jim never would condone priests breaking their vows of chastity or promises of celibacy.

A few weeks after the McCarrick revelations came the release of a devastating grand jury report in Pennsylvania, reopening the wound of clergy sex abuse in a way that hadn't happened since the *Boston Globe*'s reporting in 2002. The accounting of crimes committed and unreported in every diocese in Pennsylvania sent Catholics into an understandable frenzy. Conservatives and liberals were suddenly united, all sides calling for reform, bishop resignations, and accountability. Jim quickly wrote an article for the *New York Times* titled "The Virtues of Catholic Anger," in which he said: "In the Gospels, Jesus is described as angry many times, a stark contrast to the portrait many have of him as a doe-eyed man of peace. . . . Jesus' anger is, in a word, unselfish and constructive, intent on doing something, effecting a change."[6]

What had become the mainstream view on homosexuality as it relates to the crisis—from the 2011 study of the John Jay School of Criminal Justice ("The clinical data do not support the hypothesis that priests with a homosexual identity or those who committed same-sex sexual behavior with adults are significantly more likely to sexually abuse children than those with a heterosexual orientation or behavior.")—no longer seemed to satisfy.[7]

The conservative, Catholic, gay, political commentator Andrew Sullivan wrote an article in *New York Magazine*, "Cleansing the Catholic Church of Its Sins"; he intended these words to reestablish links between celibacy, homosexuality, and sex abuse in the church:

> Homophobia may also have increased the proportion of priests over the centuries who have been gay, because the priesthood has always been a reliable cover for not dating women. And these closeted . . . gays are the ones who may well have internalized many of the slurs against gays in the past, hated themselves, never come to terms with themselves, and seen no real difference between sexual abuse and sex. So gay priests may well have covered this stuff up for aeons, or formed cliques that perpetuated it, or developed personae that could create some campy subculture to make the awful contradictions and cruelties of sexual repression and self-loathing bearable. When no form of sex is allowed, all forms of sex can seem equally immoral.[8]

Fifteen years earlier, the same Sullivan wrote an op-ed in the *New York Times*, "Losing a Church, Keeping the Faith"

(October 19, 2003), describing himself no longer able to attend Mass given the Catholic Church's continued line on homosexuality as "intrinsically disordered."

Jim held his line, tweeting two days after Sullivan's article published at *New York Magazine*—it was August 19, 2018, the Sunday when Catholics around the United States were expecting to hear constructive words from their parish priests about significant repentance and change—"[C]learly many abusive priests were gay. But this does not mean all LGBT people are abusers, nor that all (or even most) gay priests are abusers. It's a stereotype."[9]

Less than two weeks later, after former apostolic nuncio to the United States, Archbishop Carlo Maria Viganò, published an eleven-page letter of accusations against Pope Francis, blaming the clergy abuse crisis on a "homosexual current" among clergy, Jim wrote in *America*, "The Witch Hunt for Gay Priests." He wrote: "Catholics have a right to be angry at abusive clergy, at bishops who covered up their crimes and at the sclerotic clerical system that allowed the crimes and cover-ups to go unpunished for decades. But the intensity of hate and level of anger directed at gay priests are unprecedented in my memory."

He went on to clarify some definitions that he repeatedly feels the need to address, as when using a word like "gay" to describe a priest bound by celibacy:

> What I mean by "gay priests" is ordained priests with a homosexual orientation who are living their promises of celibacy (and in religious orders, their vows of chastity). That it is necessary even to define the term "gay priest" points out the widespread misinformation about what has become perhaps the most incendiary topic in the current discussion. A few commentators have even declared that the term "gay" implies that a priest must be sexually active.

> As I use the term, a "gay priest" simply means an ordained priest who has a homosexual orientation.

He suggested what he'd been suggesting for two decades: the importance of openness about sexuality in each person's life, vows or not, and the importance of understanding one's sexuality, vows or not:

> Many priest abusers had a homosexual orientation. That is undeniable.
>
> But . . . [t]hat many abusers were gay priests does not mean that all or even most gay priests are abusers. It is a dangerous and unjust stereotype. . . .
>
> Then why does it seem like so many gay priests are abusive? One reason is that there are no public examples of the healthy, celibate gay priests to counteract these stereotypes. Why not? Because gay priests are not willing to be as public about their identity as straight priests are. For example, in a community suffering from a spate of L.G.B.T. violence, there can be no references in a Sunday homily to knowing what it is like to be bullied for being gay. The presider cannot say, "As a boy, I was bullied, too, for being gay."[10]

These would remain hot-button issues in the church worldwide.

Then Archbishop Charles Chaput of Philadelphia gave a speech at the start of the October 2018 Synod of Bishops on young people, the faith, and vocational discernment urging participants not to use any language for sexuality. He said: "there is no such thing as an 'LGBTQ Catholic' or a 'transgender Catholic' or a 'heterosexual Catholic,' as if our sexual appetites defined who we are."[11]

Three weeks later, journalist David Gibson wrote: "As Catholic leaders from around the world rush to draft a document summarizing their monthlong deliberations on reaching out to young people, they have consistently struggled with what may seem like a simple question: how to refer to gay people." Conservatives at the synod were resisting any move away from what was deemed acceptable language: "homosexual" or "same-sex attracted." Gibson quoted Jim, whom he interviewed for his article:

> If the church continues to use antiquated, outdated and overly clinical terms like "same-sex attracted" rather than the name the group uses for itself, the church will simply make dialogue more difficult and make these Catholics feel even less welcome in what is, after all, their church too. . . . Besides, if Pope Francis can use the word "gay" so can everyone else.[12]

The Synod of Bishops ended up writing in its final documents that "God loves every person and so does the Church," but they rejected any official use of the word "gay" or the acronym LGBT, unwilling to take steps toward what might appear to be affirming the sexual activity of LGBT Catholics. Jim said—on the first episode of his new "Faith in Focus" online talk show at the now newly named America Media—"The Synod decided not to use the term 'LGBT.' So, a global church that's still, in many ways, 'on the way.' "[13]

Then, Pope Francis spoke of the need for greater discernment in the vocation and formation process of homosexual priests. Whereas the pontiff had earlier declared, "Who am I to judge?" when asked about homosexual priests, at the end of 2018 he spoke of homosexuality as "fashionable" and a "mentality." Asked to clarify his views, Francis then added that we "have to urge homosexual priests, and men and women religious, to live celibacy with integrity, and above all, that they be impeccably responsible, trying to never scandalize either their communities or the faithful holy people of God."[14] Catholics at many levels seemed more confused than ever. Jim worked hard to try to allay that confusion.

* * *

Simultaneously, Jim's relationships with members of the Jesuit Curia in Rome, and with the Holy See, were deepening. In March 2017, he was appointed by Pope Francis to serve a five-year term as "consultor" to the Vatican's Secretariat for Communication, responsible for sharing and spreading the messages of the pope. The way he was appointed was typical of the Vatican's often mysterious ways of communication, perhaps pointing up the need for Jim's presence as consultor.

According to Jim:

> I found out that I was appointed early one morning over Twitter. A Vatican journalist sent me a direct message on Twitter and said, "*Complimenti!*" I said, "For what?" And he said, "You've been appointed to the Secretariat for Communication." I looked it up and there it was online. No one had told me. Then I saw all the other tweets, announcing it, and people reacting (including a few people being angry about it) and the phone started ringing. I emailed my Provincial, figuring that surely he'd know. Nope. "Congratulations!" he said. Then I emailed our Jesuit Curia in Rome, assuming that they would definitely have been told or asked. Nope. "Congratulations!" Apparently, when the Vatican appoints you to something like this, they don't need to ask![15]

A few weeks later the official notice arrived, in Latin, headed,

Summus Pontifex
FRANCISCUS.

*Consultoribus Secretariae pro Communicatione ad quin-
quennium ascripsit Reverend Patrem*

IACOBUM MARTIN, S.I.

It continued: *Id in notitiam ipsius Reverendi Patris Martin
perfertur, ut ea de re opportune certior fiat ad eiusdemque
normam se gerat.* This translates roughly to: "The Supreme
Pontiff Francis appoints as Consultor to the Secretariat for
Communication to a term of five years the Reverend Father
James Martin. This will be brought to the attention of the
Reverend Father Martin, so that it may become appropriately
clearer that he deports himself according to the proper norm."

He did so, privileged to assist Pope Francis. Jim responds
to requests from the dicastery for advice on various projects,
for example, the Pope's World Day of Communications
Message, and he travels to Rome occasionally for meetings.

This also meant that, while Jim was at the center of a
maelstrom around issues of sexuality in the church, he was
understandably calm in himself and confident of his position
with those in authority.

In one of his talks about *Building a Bridge*, at Villanova
University, Jim said: "What does respect mean? First of all,
respect means recognizing that LGBT people exist, and extending to them the same recognition that any community
deserves because of their presence among us." This language
was deliberately chosen. He then referred to (unnamed)
bishops failing to mention the existence of LGBT Catholics,
failing to acknowledge tragedies involving LGBT people,
and not "helping LGBT Catholics feel like they are part of
the Church—because they are."[16]

Protests at such lectures, and abusive comments against him online, may continue to follow Jim for the rest of his life. He shows a remarkable calmness about this. "I know that as a Jesuit and as a priest, I always want to be charitable and loving. That's the first requirement of anything that I write, or speak, or tweet," he remarked in public conversation with journalist Ross Douthat—and almost without exception, there would be no disagreements with this quality in Jim, even among his detractors.[17]

Several years earlier, he had written the following in a "Prayer for Frustrated Catholics":

> I need your help, God. . . . Help me to understand that there was never a time when there were not arguments or disputes within your church. . . . Give me wisdom.
>
> . . . Help me to be peaceful when people tell me that I don't belong in the church, that I'm a heretic for trying to make things better or that I'm not a good Catholic. I know that I was baptized. You called me by name to be in your church, God. As long as I draw breath, help me remember how the holy waters of baptism welcomed me into your holy family of sinners and saints. Let the voice that called me into your church be what I hear when other voices tell me that I'm not welcome in the church. Give me peace.[18]

He has often said that politics is not his domain but also that he doesn't mind "afflicting the comfortable," to use Dorothy Day's phrase, when his applications of the Gospel to current events show him taking political sides. This is nothing new. Twenty-five years earlier, in the pages of *America*, he'd be "political" when it seemed necessary. For example: "So while it is no longer acceptable (as in the Age of Reagan) to push a product simply because it's flashy or chic, if we can appeal to a shallow sense of 'spirituality,' we can make it more respectable. . . . Who needs prayer? Buy a car."[19] Then, two years later, taking on Microsoft founder Bill Gates, who was profiled in a cover story in *Time*: "[I]s anyone else getting tired of magazine articles about Bill Gates? . . . It is as if his immense wealth blinds the media from being the least bit critical of him."[20] Excessive wealth was much of what Jim focused on then, in the decades before "LGBT" was even part of the vocabulary.

"Jesus was always reaching out to those on the margins," he said in a Facebook Live conversation, adding that that was the impulse prompting much of his work.

He faces daily, sometimes hourly, criticism from far-right quarters of Catholic Twitter and angry "traditionalist" Catholics. A sample of repeated accusations include these from Amazon.com reader reviews: "If you're Catholic, read and follow the Catechism. Don't waste your money on this book."

And, "It's rather odd that a book ostensibly on a Catholic approach to a sensitive topic never once mentions what the Church teaches about that topic, which curious readers will find in the Catechism of the Catholic Church's treatment of the Sixth Commandment (paragraphs 2331–2359). Instead, Martin assumes unquestioningly that same sex attraction is a gift if an individual deems it to be so."

And, "He is not teaching what the Catholic Church teaches about homosexual acts. Read the Catechism if you want to know what the Catholic Church teaches. This book annoyed me—he writes as though compassion, charity, sensitivity are NEW ideas! The church teaches us to show compassion, charity and sensitivity to ALL people. But the church does not condone sin and homosexual acts are sin. Love the sinner—hate the sin!"[21]

Sometimes, links were even suggested between abusers and Jim, and in the most tangential ways. For example, in

June 2018 after Cardinal McCarrick was removed from public ministry by the Holy See, stories continued to multiply of the alleged abuse, including one on the front page of the *New York Times*. Then Matthew Schmitz, a senior editor at conservative Catholic magazine *First Things*, tweeted an *ad hominem* attack: "Rod Dreher reports that Cardinal Kevin Farrell and Joseph Tobin, both of whom have endorsed @JamesMartinSJ's book, are proteges of Cardinal McCarrick."[22] Such an outrageous statement was welcomed by the increasingly divided right wing in the church.

Characteristically, Jim did not comment directly. He did, however, publish a series of tweets addressing the conversation online and elsewhere about the connection between McCarrick's abuse—which was aimed at members of his own sex—and claims that homosexuality and homosexual priests are to blame for sex abuse in the Catholic Church. Jim wrote:

> The connection between sex abuse and homosexuality in the Catholic priesthood, in light of the Cardinal McCarrick case, and some ill-informed and outright homophobic comments:

> Being gay (or, more broadly, being LGBT) does not make a person a pedophile, an ephebophile, or any kind of sex abuser. How do we know this?

> Answer: the example of millions of emotionally healthy and psychologically mature LGBT people who have never abused anyone—and never will abuse anyone.

> Moreover, the example of the many healthy, faithful, dedicated gay priests who live out their promises of celibacy and vows of chastity and are beloved by their parishioners. I know scores of them.

Then why does it seem like such a high percentage of gay priests are abusers? Because healthy celibate gay priests are usually not permitted to be open about their sexuality. (There are exceptions: Fathers Fred Daley in Syracuse and Gregory Greiten in Milwaukee.)

Why are most of them not "out"? There are many reasons. Often their bishops or religious superiors will not give them permission; they are private people; or they are afraid (usually of stereotyping of the kind I'm discussing).

Thus, in the absence of any other examples, the only (or predominant) public examples of gay priests end up being notorious abusers, like Cardinal McCarrick.[23]

Back in November 2000, Jim had acknowledged in *America* that "homosexuality is defined by church teaching as a 'strong tendency ordered toward an intrinsic moral evil' ('The Pastoral Care of Homosexual Persons,' 1986)" and "The current teaching of the church on homosexuality is clear: Homosexual acts are 'intrinsically disordered' (*Catechism of the Catholic Church*, No. 2357), and even a homosexual orientation is an 'objective disorder'"—the sort of acknowledgments his critics between 2017 and 2019 kept reminding him of. But then he added this as central to the message of *Building a Bridge*:

> But the church also teaches that a homosexual person "must be accepted with respect, compassion and sensitivity" (*Catechism*, No. 2358).

* * *

Some friends of Jim were particularly helpful to him during these years. As he has since the novitiate, he meets regularly with a small group of Jesuit friends for "faith sharing," where they talk about their experiences of God in their daily ministry and prayer and offer support for one another. But while most of his close friends are in the Society of Jesus, not all are.

One is Kevin Ahern, a professor of theology at Manhattan College. The two men share an interest in old Catholic religious communities and sometimes take daylong road trips to the Hudson Valley, to explore and poke around old religious order houses, monasteries, retreat houses, and convents. "We're the only ones who seem to like this!" Jim once told me. Then, a few months after *Building a Bridge* came out, and the attacks started coming in fast and furious, there were few people who were as supporting and caring in that period as Kevin.

Driving in the car one day on one of their mini-pilgrimages, Jim got a phone call from someone apologetically telling him that one of his talks was going to be cancelled. Kevin and Jim were together in the car, and Kevin pulled over to the side of the road, as Jim put the call on speaker phone. After Jim hung up, he was able to vent a bit and talk about the way forward with a friend. Jim found it providential that they were together at that moment, and Ahern has become an even better friend, a "real brother," as Jim describes him.[24]

There is also Jim's old church history professor, Sister Janice Farnham, who has become a wisdom figure for him. When he was at Weston studying theology, she met Jim's parents during their visit for his diaconate ordination, and they fell in love with her—"as everyone does who knows her," Jim says. And when Jim's father was diagnosed with cancer in 2000, it was Sister Janice who helped Jim accept the road that God was laying out for him—loving, caring for, and accompanying James Sr. in his last months. Jim explained to me:

> She said, "Can you surrender to the future that God has in store for you?" I use that question often with people now. And she did one of the kindest things anyone has ever done for me: In my dad's last few weeks on earth, she took a train all the way from Boston to Philadelphia, on her extremely limited sister's budget, somehow found a place at a nearby convent, stayed overnight, and visited my dad in the hospital the next day to say Goodbye. A few hours later she got back on the train and went home to Boston. It meant so much to my dad and to my family and to me.[25]

She continues to be one of his closest friends.

And then there is Ivan Briggeler. Ivan and his family, originally from Argentina, are longtime parishioners at St. Ignatius in New York City and have been extremely supportive of Jim. Ivan was for a time one of Jim's spiritual directees, but their relationship has moved beyond this. As Jim explained to me, Ivan and his family's support came recently in the most extraordinary way:

> Two years ago, he told me that he suspected that his son Marcos, then a high school junior, might be gay. Ivan and Maria are amazing parents, and I told him not to worry: all they had to do was love Marcos. Not long afterwards Marcos came out to me, and of course to his parents and his siblings, who accepted him with open arms. Then, just a few months later, when New Ways Ministry invited me to give a talk on LGBT Catholics, which would later become the basis for *Building a Bridge*, Ivan and Marcos decided that they were going to accompany me to the event. I couldn't believe it. The talk was in Baltimore, and I told them that wasn't necessary. But they insisted. So they

drove me all the way down from New York, a four or five hour trip, stayed in a hotel, came to the talk (where Marcos was the youngest person there), and then drove me all the way back in a driving rainstorm. Honestly, I'm still amazed they did that.[26]

Later on, Ivan helped to start an LGBT outreach program in their parish in Manhattan. Ivan is someone that Jim can rely on completely. They speak to one another, says Jim, like brothers.

* * *

The outpouring of response to *Building a Bridge* did not translate easily into book sales. Thirteen months in and sales were only 15,590 copies according to Nielsen BookScan, an industry data provider that counts copies purchased at major retailers, online and brick-and-mortar. BookScan does not include copies purchased at Catholic shops. Eighteen weeks after the release of the second edition, sales according to BookScan were just 3,704.

These numbers were uncommon for a James Martin book. His popularity was at its zenith before *Building a Bridge. My Life with the Saints*, for instance, had sold 118,762 copies to date across three editions as of the day when these *Bridge* numbers were accessed.[27] And if BookScan counted copies sold through Catholic retailers, that number would have easily doubled for *My Life with the Saints*—which could not be said for *Building a Bridge*. Some Catholic booksellers would not stock it. And many parishes and colleges hosting Jim's talks were often purchasing *Bridge* in bulk directly from the publisher (such sales going unrecorded by BookScan).

Nevertheless, Jim's editor says that they never expected to reach Jim's full audience with the book, which was, in point of fact, about a very specific topic with a limited appeal.[28] That full audience, now, is also fragmented.

But the effect of *Bridge* on the church's understanding and perception of LGBT people has been undeniable.

It can't be a coincidence that the papal office and Curia seem to have been tracking with Jim during this time. Pope Francis made headlines in May 2018 when it was widely reported he told a gay man how he doesn't care if he's gay, and neither does God.

A few days later, *The Tablet*'s correspondent in Rome, Christopher Lamb, tweeted: "About to appear on @bbcworldservice to discuss #Pope's reported remarks to Juan Carlos Cruz, a gay man, that God 'made you like that and loves you like that.' The major change under this papacy is the language now being used in Rome about gay people."

At that time, Jim did not believe that Pope Francis had seen a copy of his book, but the pope seems to have been following its message.[29] Later on, he would receive assurances of the pope's support through intermediaries.

Then, on June 11, 2018, a headline at *America*'s website stunned even savvy Catholics and veteran Vatican watchers: "Father James Martin to speak on welcoming L.G.B.T. Catholics at World Meeting of Families."

The organizers of that worldwide gathering, including Cardinal Kevin Farrell, prefect of the Vatican's Dicastery for Laity, Family, and Life, the World Meeting of Families' chief organizer, set to take place in Ireland, had extended a surprise invitation to Jim. Farrell was also an early endorser of *Bridge*. It was an unmistakable sign of Vatican approval of his book.

The surprise invitation, which delighted Jim's supporters and infuriated his critics, followed what you might call a "pushback to the pushback," which included several prominent

US cardinals and bishops pointedly standing up for Jim's book and his burgeoning ministry to LGBT Catholics. Bishop Robert McElroy of San Diego penned a strong defense of Jim in the pages of *America*, arguing that the virulent attacks on him "expose a cancer in the church."[30] Cardinal Blase Cupich, the influential archbishop of Chicago and close associate of Pope Francis, invited Jim to give two lectures at Holy Name Cathedral during Lent 2018. The next year, Archbishop Wilton Gregory of Atlanta (later named archbishop of Washington, DC) would publicly invite Jim to give several speeches in his archdiocese. The Vatican invitation, though, outshone them all in terms of "pushback to the pushback."

Jim said in *America*, "The organizers have asked me to speak about how parishes can welcome L.G.B.T. Catholics, as well as their parents and families. So I hope to share 'best practices' from parishes that have successfully reached out to the L.G.B.T. Catholic community."[31]

What he didn't say was that this would be the first time the Vatican had sanctioned a talk on LGBT Catholics. The talk went on as planned, despite a petition campaign started by members of Tradition, Family and Property, a traditionalist Catholic movement founded in Brazil in 1960, that garnered more than ten thousand signatures and was publicized by the conservative *Catholic Herald* magazine and others in the United Kingdom and Ireland.[32]

Then, on June 19, the Vatican used the term "LGBT" for the first time, acknowledging the existence of LGBT young people in the working document for the Fifteenth Ordinary General Assembly of the Synod of Bishops set to meet October 3–28, 2018. In that document, "Young People, the Faith and Vocational Discernment," the Vatican wrote: "Some LGBT youth . . . wish to benefit from greater closeness and experience greater care by the Church."[33] Later on that term would be used again in the title of Jim's talk, a title that the Vatican itself chose: "Showing Respect and Welcome in our Parishes to LGBT People and Their Families."

And on August 2, when Pope Francis spoke of his intention to rewrite the catechism, amending a teaching of Pope John Paul II, to make it clear the death penalty is always wrong—"inadmissible," in Francis's words—and adding that Catholics worldwide should be actively working to abolish its practice, David Gibson of Fordham University tweeted: "BTW the teaching behind Pope Francis' move to declare death penalty inadmissible in all cases is same teaching behind Catholicism's teaching on abortion. And in support of dignity of LGBT people."[34]

In the end, what struck many people about Jim during this turbulent period was the calm with which he seemed to face his detractors. Some of this can be attributed to his experience on retreat, where he felt Jesus invite him to let go of the need to be "loved, liked or even approved of," as he put it. Other things contributed to this calm, as he recently explained to me:

> That moment during the retreat was transformative for me. It invited me to let go of the need for people to like me. But the vitriol directed at me was something new. Eventually though, I realized something: I had the backing of my Jesuit superiors, "100 percent," as my Jesuit Provincial told me, and my Jesuit brothers, except for maybe one or two. I had the backing of the Jesuit Superior General, who had communicated his support through Jesuit channels. This was essential for me, and helped me relax about the pushback. Also, I knew that many cardinals, archbishops and bishops supported me, both publicly and privately, especially those I admired. Eventually, I knew that I even

had the support of the pope. Then I knew from visiting parishes and colleges around the country that I had the support of many, if not most Catholics in the pews, especially LGBT people and their families and friends.

At the same time, I started to see that some of the angriest voices online were people who just seemed homophobic and hateful. So why would I care about that? Legitimate criticism and questions are one thing, but pure hatred is another. And what kind of Jesuit would I be if I let that kind of hatred dissuade me from reaching out to a group that feels itself on the margins? What kind of Jesuit would I be if I didn't love them?

Gradually something happened to me, something that I had been asking for in prayer probably since I entered the novitiate: the gift of what we Jesuits call "detachment" or "indifference." In common parlance, it means freedom. And, one day, someone sent me some hateful online column attacking me, and I looked at it and realized, "I don't care." It didn't bother me. It was something of a surprise, too, since I'd been someone who at one time was focused on getting people to like me. But now I felt free of the need for his approval. So now my mantra is, about all the hatred directed my way, "Who cares?"

I'm confident in this ministry not only because of the backing I have from superiors and from most of the Catholic faithful, but also because I think this is what Jesus is inviting me to do at this point in my life. And I feel like I've been given the "grace of indifference," as we say, to help me do it. It only took thirty years for that grace to arrive, but I'm grateful that it did.

CHAPTER NINE

Priest in the Media

In Kenya, I often saw sheep who recognized their shepherd's voice. How do we know God's "voice"? In general, when we're progressing spiritually: it's calm, consoling, encouraging, removing obstacles. When we're going backwards spiritually: fierce, shocking, challenging.

—James Martin, SJ, tweet, April 24, 2018

After the success of several bestselling books, and with his face a fixture on television, Jim seemed to become the priest on record for every story related to the Catholic Church. As early as 2009, he was being quoted in national media on everything from the "large-hearted, compassionate, pastoral, sensitive, and above all, Christian" gesture of Cardinal Sean O'Malley to preside at the Funeral Mass of Senator Edward Kennedy, to how comedian Sarah Silverman with her snarky "Sell the Vatican. Feed the world" comment wasn't to be dismissed: "[I]n her postmodern, potty-mouthed way [perhaps she] is on to something. Like Jesus was. Sell the Vatican? Well, maybe not everything but perhaps a statue or two?"[1]

From interviews in the immediate aftermath of the 9/11 tragedy, answering questions about God, evil, and vengeance, to scrutiny on the subject of clergy sex abuse, beginning also in the early 2000s, Jim had shown himself capable of handling the spotlight. Then, with the controversy of *Building a Bridge*, one result for his public ministry was a thorough evolution from the jocular and popular "Official Chaplain of *The Colbert Report*" back to the Jesuit on the front lines.

As a public figure, Martin addressed nearly every controversial or burning issue involving religion and public policy over the first two decades of this century. Saturday morning, April 28, 2018, for instance he tweeted:

> RIP #AlfieEvans. Baptized, sinless, and made in the image and likeness of the God, he has been welcomed into eternal life. Please pray for his young parents, his doctors, and all who loved and cared for him. He is now praying for us.

Ignore the typo in the second sentence; tweets are often typed rapidly. Alfie Evans is largely forgotten now, but his case was front-page news in early 2018. His parents carried on a very public, bitter dispute with the Liverpool hospital where Alfie lay in a vegetative state over whether to end the infant's life support. Alfie's father solicited the support of Pope Francis, and the couple sought to remove Alfie to a hospital in Rome. The infant's death had been reported just minutes before Martin sent out his message.

Several months earlier, the inauguration of Donald J. Trump as US president led to a range of opportunities in Jim's ministry as a priest on call in the media. The new president's anti-immigrant campaign made that all but certain. By election day, on November 8, 2016, Jim's prayer—published online at *America*—spoke for religious progressives everywhere:

> God, I know that I don't have to get angry.
> I don't have to get worked up.
> I don't have to get depressed.
>
> I just have to use
> my conscience
> and vote.
>
> So help me to remember
> what Jesus taught in the Gospels,
> and what our church teaches,
> especially about the unborn, the poor,
> the refugee, the migrant,
> the sick, the homeless,
> the disabled, the hungry,
> the elderly and the lonely.
>
> Help me to remember the "least" among us,
> and help me ponder in my heart
> how to cast my vote for the good of all.
>
> God, I know that no candidate is perfect,
> because I'm not perfect either,
> the last time I checked.
> So free me of the burden of having to
> vote for someone who satisfies
> all my desires for a candidate.
> My candidate will be imperfect,
> like me.
>
> Help me to be grateful for the ability to vote,
> because not everyone has that privilege.
> Help me to be at peace after I vote, too.

And when I meet people voting for someone else,
help me to take a deep breath and
give them the benefit of the doubt,
because they are following their consciences, too.

Help me to remember
that even though they sometimes drive me nuts,
I don't have to argue with them,
I don't have to convince them,
I don't have to hate them,
And I don't have to demonize them.

Then, after the election, help me work for unity.
Because I know that's what you want.

Amen.[2]

* * *

These weren't new themes for Jim, who had been writing about the needs of migrants and refugees since his days in East Africa in the early 1990s. One of his television reviews from 1996 was titled with the verse from Exodus 22:20: "You Shall Not Oppress an Alien." It was about the 1.5 million refugees that fled Mozambique during its fifteen-year civil war that ended in 1993.

To this theme, and often to that verse, Jim would return, starting in 2016—when politicians talked of building a wall on the southern border between the United States and Mexico. Jim was there to remind people that "the whole thrust of the Old and New Testaments, when it comes to migrants and refugees, is that we're supposed to welcome them."[3]

Jim is always looking for ways to protect the vulnerable. A feature in *America* ten years after the piece on Mozambique refugees even took on the subject of Judas Iscariot, seeking to remove stigmas associated with one of the most notorious figures in human history. In the end, Jim found that Judas may have been a lot like most of us: "Why did Judas do it? Probably because Judas, like most of us, wanted to make God in his own image—rather than the other way around."[4]

* * *

Political issues were suddenly impossible to avoid. For example, in the early hours of December 2, 2017, the Republican-controlled US Senate passed a controversial tax reform bill that had been denounced by the USCCB and most every Catholic voice for justice, including Jim's, in the days leading up to a vote.

That morning, around breakfast time, Jim tweeted in a tone befitting his usual directness, but without any conciliatory possibility; he was angry:

> The US will soon face the consequences of a #TaxBill that takes money from the poor to give to the rich. Those who voted for it will face consequences later, when they are judged. Do you think Jesus's words about being judged on how we care for the poor don't apply? Think again.

It was retweeted by more than four thousand people that day. Some were fellow Catholics unhappy with what Jim had said. William Dailey, CSC, an American priest who was director of the Newman Center for Faith and Reason at the University of Notre Dame's campus in Dublin, Ireland, retweeted it, adding: "It's fine for a priest to take a position on legislation. It is forbidden to take a line on the souls of legislators. By Jesus, in fact." When I asked Jim if his religious superiors were bothered by what he had done, he replied, "Not at all! I assume that my superiors believe in the Final Judgment!"[5]

He sees these responses as an essential part of his ministry, as a member of the Catholic media, a priest, and a Jesuit. Also, since his Jesuit ministry began, he has looked for those who need protecting, uplifting, rehabilitating, and healing. He has always had a gift for finding the one who needs lifting up and then doing the lifting. Much of this, as he often says, came from his Jesuit formation, when he worked with, among others, the sick and dying in Mother Teresa's hospice in Jamaica, street-gang members in Chicago, inmates in Boston, and, most of all, East African refugees in the slums of Nairobi. Jesuit formation not only requires young Jesuits to work with poor populations, all the way from the novitiate to Final Vows, but also invites them to accompany them and advocate for them.

Issues and controversies of the moment that involve Catholics or the Catholic Church invariably receive a comment from him—even if it might involve controversy. He seeks permission from his boss at America Media or his provincial if he is to appear on television or radio or be interviewed on any hot-button topic. That is part of his vow of obedience, but it is also a recognition that anything any Jesuit says reflects on the Society of Jesus.

* * *

His defense of the poor and marginalized has positioned Jim as a liberal, or progressive, in the ideological landscape. He identifies with Pedro Arrupe, SJ, the former superior general of the Society (1965–1983), and his directing of the Jesuits to carry out the church's ministry of "preferential option for the poor." In this way, for example, Jim often advocated, during the papacies of John Paul II and Benedict XVI, for the canonization of Archbishop Óscar Romero, who was assassinated as he lifted the chalice to consecrate the wine while celebrating Mass in San Salvador in 1980.

Such positions, in those years, pigeonholed Jim, as did his role at *America* magazine, which was often viewed on the "left" of the religious spectrum. So be it, Jim might say, if that's what you call preaching the Gospel of Christ.

With the papacy of Pope Francis, beginning in March 2013, the tide of the church would change in ways that made Jim's views much more mainstream. Óscar Romero was beatified in 2015 and canonized three years later. Also in 2018, the superior general of the Society of Jesus, Arturo Sosa, SJ, announced the start of the process toward beatification for Pedro Arrupe. But then, the "traditionalist" response of Catholics who had felt comforted in their views under the last two popes began to retrench and refuse to acknowledge that a change of emphasis and view from the Holy See was acceptable, or even possible. This is the environment that Jim works under today.

He can't, however, be easily tagged as a liberal in the church without regard for conservative issues. The topics of his writing point to this: he's written a hundredfold more on sainthood, prayer, and vocation than on welcoming gays. His faithfulness to his vows, including obedience, has been unfaltering.

There was the time, for instance, when novelist Dan Brown's blockbuster novel, *The Da Vinci Code* was turned into a blockbuster film. Jim had written eleven years earlier, "Opus Dei in the United States," an article highly critical of the prelature, leading to criticism from many quarters. But he was also one to come to Opus Dei's defense when they were maltreated by Dan Brown and Hollywood.

It was Jim who wrote in *America* as the movie was selling to long lines of moviegoers: "It is difficult to understand how a bestselling novelist and a mainstream director [Ron Howard] could get away with such public defamation of a real organization. Equally disturbing is the manner in which Mr. Brown is typically presented (and presents himself) in the media as an expert whose historical research has 'revealed' heretofore unknown facts that are supposedly cleverly disguised in the book and film as fiction."[6]

Even more important for people of faith, Jim recently wrote for an article for *America* that was widely shared, titled "The Literal Flesh-and-Blood Resurrection Is the Heart of My Faith."[7] That is not the talk of theological liberalism.

* * *

Public exposure and moderate fame have led to other opportunities as well. Spiritual direction, for example, remains an essential part of Jim's ministry, and it is a ministry that is meant to be private. Occasionally, however, an interviewer or journalist will reveal that a famous person—actor Andrew Garfield, for instance—is seeing Jim for spiritual direction, but the substance of these relationships is like the confessional, not to be discussed.

Some of Jim's guidance to those he sees for direction is occasionally shared with wider audiences. When he began to offer the weekly podcast *The Examen*, for example, these short messages often included such advice. One from late 2018 included a core Jesuit teaching, and one that Jim loves to share:

> Over the past few weeks, we've been talking about the kinds of experiences that can happen in prayer, which is

often a source of confusion for even devout Christians. Many people wonder: What happens when I close my eyes? Or, what is supposed to happen? Well, one of the most common experiences is the revelation of desires. And I don't mean mere surface desires and wants like "I want a new laptop" or "I want a new car" or "I want a new apartment." No, I mean deeper desires, the longings that draw you closer to God, and help you become the person God means for you to be.

For example, you might be praying about a Gospel passage and suddenly feel an urge to follow Jesus more closely. That is, while praying you may experience a powerful attraction to the person of Jesus. You want to know more about him, read more about him, and spend more time praying about him. Where do these desires come from? From God. Now, not every desire that arises in prayer is from God. You have to discern, too, to see what makes sense and what fits in terms of what you know about God. But something like a desire to follow Christ is clearly coming from God. St. Ignatius Loyola, founder of the Jesuits would agree. After all, he sometimes asked people to pray an unusual prayer: a prayer to understand their deepest desires.[8]

He is gradually becoming a more frequent face on the big screen as well. Jim's first appearance in a major motion picture came in director Martin Scorsese's most expensive film ever, *The Irishman*, starring Al Pacino and Robert De Niro and produced by Netflix. Pacino plays Jimmy Hoffa, and De Niro plays the Irish hitman who confessed to murdering the famous labor leader. Principal filming ended in March 2018, and Jim was called on by his friend "Marty" to perform two baptisms, in Latin, portraying a priest from the 1950s. Actors De Niro and Joe Pesci were both on set that day.

A documentary has also been filmed about Jim, focusing on the work of *Building a Bridge*, by filmmakers Evan Mascagni and Shannon Post. The film focuses on the dramatic progress on LGBT issues in the United States and around the world, despite intolerance still found in much of organized religion. Mascagni and Post, with Nick Capezzera, director of photography, spent hundreds of hours with Jim at his public talks, in interviews, and filming the stories of people whose lives have intersected in emotional and spiritual ways with Jim's message of acceptance and welcome. Filming was completed in the summer of 2019.[9]

And then there is Jim's new internet television show, the already-mentioned "Faith in Focus." On October 18, 2018, the first episode premiered at America Media. The idea originated with Matt Malone, SJ, Jim's boss, and Jim showed initial reluctance, fearing the perception of something akin to "The James Martin Show!" But when the concept was adjusted to be a way to profile the faith of other people, Jim took to liking it. The studio at America Media was built after the move to their new office suite in 2016 and has also been used by Jim for other projects, including his Examen podcasts and for recording podcasts to be presented to audiences to which Jim would not be traveling in person. Jim and Jeannie Gaffigan were the first guests on the monthly show; another was his old friend Stephen Colbert; and, later, one of his favorite theologians, Elizabeth Johnson, CSJ, appeared. The main topic of each conversation was something that has engrossed Jim ever since the novitiate: Who is God for you?

CHAPTER TEN

Humility, Prayer, Lazarus

The third level of humility, the highest, is when a person is able to choose something dishonorable because it brings him or her closer to Christ. "I desire to be regarded as a useless fool for Christ, who before me was regarded as such," in the words of the *Spiritual Exercises*. A person accepts being misunderstood, perhaps by everyone, just as Christ was.

—James Martin, SJ[1]

Back during his theology studies at Weston Jesuit School of Theology, in the spring of 1996, Jim was diagnosed with a repetitive strain injury: tendinitis in both hands and wrists (carpal tunnel syndrome), the sort of injury one receives from too much typing at keyboards. By this time, he was a memoirist, so he began to mention his malady and how it allowed him to understand people forced to deal with chronic pain and who suffer silently in other ways. He wrote:

Feeling compassion for others can dramatically increase when you're in pain. I've found myself much more solicitous of the elderly, the infirm, the disabled and homeless men and women on the street. For this I am thankful. Suffering, I think, makes one more Christian. It's a strange thing really, but painful experiences can open up your heart more than you would ever expect. I would imagine that it was the same with Jesus, "a man of suffering well acquainted with infirmity," as Isaiah foretold (53:3). More to the point, St. Paul writes that because Jesus suffered, he wonderfully understands our suffering (Heb. 2:18).[2]

A similar article appeared in *The Tablet*, the Catholic weekly published from London, England. "[H]ow very alone sufferers can feel," he wrote there, "a theme that often crops up in Scripture. It's difficult to communicate exactly what's going on with your body and inside your head. And one sometimes feels, during the worst moments, that God is far away."[3]

While at Weston, Jim was expected to take notes during theology lectures, and he had written exams. As we've seen, he was also putting his experience in Kenya to writerly use, producing articles for *America*, *Review for Religious*, *Catholic Digest*, and other publications. He would borrow fellow students' lecture notes and often replace written exams with oral ones, but there was still *This Our Exile*, his memoir about East Africa, to produce. Most often, he put off the work to moments when his hands and wrists hurt less, but there were also friends who helped input edits and changes and occasionally typed while Jim dictated.

A decade later, he would confide about his carpal tunnel in the context of an article about the "American Lourdes," the Catholic shrine at Chimayo in New Mexico: "Each year when I am invited to accompany the Order of Malta on their trip to Lourdes, I pray for healing. Yet each year I find that my hands have gotten no better. (On the other hand, they've gotten no worse.)"[4] His book, *Lourdes Diary: Seven*

Days at the Grotto of Massabieille, had just published twenty months earlier.

It was a small book, sandwiched between lots of other work, but his visit to Lourdes, the first of several over the years as a chaplain with the Order of Malta, had a profound effect on Jim. He recently explained to me:

> I was tremendously moved by Lourdes—by the story, by the place, by the faith of the people. And I fully believe the story of the apparitions to St. Bernadette Soubirous. One day, there was an invitation for some people in our group to assist in the baths, that is, to help the infirm in and out of the sunken baths into which water from the spring Bernadette discovered is directed. It's the main reason people come to Lourdes. Being somewhat self-centered, I wondered if helping out in the baths would be physically difficult or even if I'd pull a muscle. I was still a bit of a hypochondriac, then, and too focused on my physical well-being. But I said yes anyway.
>
> Not surprisingly, it was a moving experience working with four or five other men who couldn't communicate except for gestures. (In each compartment they had one individual who speaks French, one Spanish, one German and one English.) Even though it was heavy work, and there was a lot of grunting on everyone's part, we ended up helping everyone, including some very heavy people, into the tubs. The next day I woke up wondering if I'd be at all sore, and I gingerly got out of bed. And then the strangest thing happened. I usually stretch in the morning, and I'm pretty tight and can barely reach my toes. But that morning when I sat down and tried to reach my toes, I was able to bend my face all the way to my knees and reach my hands way past my feet. I couldn't believe it. It was like God, or Mary, was saying, "Don't worry, I've got you." And that's never happened since.[5]

* * *

Living with pain as a young Jesuit taught Jim humility. He was forced to abide the malady for two more decades. He also experienced his own frailty in the stomach problems that plagued him in the final months of his employment at General Electric. This too was a sort of stress injury. And in both Jamaica and East Africa, during the novitiate and regency, there were some days of intense loneliness and longing. To know Jim is to witness intelligence, wit, and humor and also the full range of human emotion and experience.

Still, nothing could have fully prepared him for the exercise in humility that his dogged message to the church to become accepting of LGBT people made for him. He has been a target for so many people who are unhappy with the church for a variety of reasons. He set out to support what he saw as the most marginalized group in the church when the pontificate of Pope Francis seemed to have created a "Kairos moment," in Jim's estimation, when "something was shifting in the Church."[6] But then that rapidly changed. Ideological sides were drawn. In a few far-right quarters, which might have embraced his prior books, Jim's reputation is now seen as compromised. He has been insulted regularly. Reflecting on the quotation that leads this chapter, one might assume that Jim set out to practice the Third Degree of Humility, according to Ignatian spirituality, by writing *Building a Bridge*. He didn't. He told me:

> I try to strive for the Third Degree in all that I do, but I didn't realize when I started writing [the book] that it would evoke such strong reactions—both positive and negative. So I didn't set out to "humble myself" in any way, unless it was unconsciously. I just set out to do what I thought was the right thing to do.[7]

It must have been a time in his life when courage and con-templation were essential. Despite this, his friends have often remarked that he had a peace about him that was uncanny.

And he has kept his sense of humor. In late March 2019, while accepting The Thomas A. Dooley Award for his faith-based LGBT compassion and leadership from the Gay and Lesbian Alumni of the University of Notre Dame and Saint Mary's College, Jim said by video: "I'm very proud of this honor. Now, the Jesuits are not supposed to be proud at all, or at least not *too* proud. We sometimes like to say, 'The Jesuits are number one in all things, including humility,' " to much laughter.[8]

* * *

The work of becoming LGBT accepting in the church may continue for many years. To date, there aren't even many Catholic priests, deacons, religious, and lay leaders who have been willing or able to reveal their full identity to their congregations.

"This man is a pioneer," Jim tweeted the morning of De-cember 18, 2017, linking to a *National Catholic Reporter* online opinion piece by Fr. Gregory Grieten of the Archdio-cese of Milwaukee in which the priest, after twenty-five years of ordained priestly ministry, revealed that he was homosexual in orientation. Jim went on: "There are hun-dreds, if not thousands, of celibate gay priests in the Catholic Church, offering their lives to God and God's people. The church is invited to see, and accept this truth. Because the truth sets us free." Jim's response was uncommon among priests, in showing public support for Grieten. Grieten's own archbishop, Jerome Listecki of Milwaukee, also showed support the following day, with some caveats:

We support Father Greiten in his own, personal journey and telling his story of coming to understand and live with his sexual orientation. As the Church teaches, those with same sex attraction must be treated with understanding and compassion. My preference would have been not to publicly announce this because it can be confusing for some people as to whether someone with same sex attraction can minister as a priest. However, as priests who have made a promise and commitment to celibacy, we know that every week there are people in our pews who struggle with the question of homosexuality. Fr. Greg's own story reminds each of us of God's call to continue to grow in understanding and to live holy, chaste lives.[9]

Jim continues to face anger from some right-wing Catholics who see a sort of "red line" not to be crossed on the issues he is addressing. Some comments that particularly raised the ire of these ideological opponents were Jim playfully saying he'd like to canonize Sr. Jeannine Gramick.[10] Gramick was an early advocate for acceptance of gays and lesbians in the church, and in 1984 the Vatican's Congregation for Institutes of Consecrated Life and for Societies of Apostolic Life ordered her to cease pastoral care of homosexual persons without faithfully presenting the church's teaching on homosexuality. Fifteen years later, Sr. Jeannine's ministry was forbidden by the Congregation for the Doctrine of the Faith. Then, when her religious congregation forbade her to speak on gay rights, she refused, and left for another congregation.

But Jim feels he is on the right course in his ministry of outreach to LGBT people and in his insistence that the Catholic Church begin to welcome them as equals to heterosexual people in every aspect of life and ministry. He received confirmation of this in September 2019, when Pope Francis invited Jim to a thirty-minute private audience in the Apostolic Palace to encourage his LGBT ministry. The appointment, covered extensively in the worldwide media, was published on the Vatican's official calendar, an unmistakable sign of papal support.

* * *

There will surely be many more James Martin books to come. Most recently, he's turned his attention back to prayer, a topic he's discussed in many of his writings.

For twenty years, he had recommended the Jesuit William A. Barry's *God and You* (1987) to anyone who asked him what was best to read on the subject of prayer. It was Barry—rector of the Jesuit Community at Boston College when Jim was a novice in the New England Province—who taught Jim about "prayer as a personal relationship." That, in fact, is the subtitle of the book that Jim handed out to people for two decades. Looking on prayer as a relationship is the way to overcome most every hesitation that keeps people from praying, Jim would say, most of all, lack of time. You would make time to be with a good friend. God is that friend, and more.

But Fr. Barry's book is very brief and without many examples and practices for people to put this wisdom to use. This is one reason why Jim finally decided to write a book on prayer himself. As he was finishing the writing, I asked him for other reasons:

> My hope for the book on prayer is that it's a user-friendly
> guide to something that tends to baffle a lot of people. My
> main goal is to answer the questions, "How can I pray?"
> and also "What goes on when I pray?" So many people
> wonder, basically, "What happens when I close my eyes?"
> So I'll try to offer not only different ways of prayer but talk
> about the fruits of prayer: insights, emotions, memories,

desires, feelings, words, images, and so on. I find that a great many books on prayer assume that people already "get" what's supposed to happen when they pray, when in my experience that's what many people are most confused about. I want this book to be something you can give to anyone, even someone who feels that prayer is not for them. Or that they "can't pray." In the same way that *The Jesuit Guide* tried to make Ignatian spirituality accessible to all, this new book aims to do that with prayer.[11]

In the introduction to *Learning to Pray*, he summarizes what he sees as "Ten Reasons Believers Don't Pray." Number ten is: "They fear change. When people start to pray, they sometimes wonder, What will happen if I keep praying? Sometimes they worry that they'll become religious fanatics. (Unlikely, I say.) Or that God will invite them to do something outlandish, like give up everything they own and quit their jobs to work full time with the poor. (Also unlikely, but then again, who knows?) Finally, they think that perhaps God will invite them to some sort of change. (Likely.)"

It can't be an accident that this tenth of ten principles—in a book that was a long time coming for this Jesuit—provides almost a summary of his own experience of not praying, facing scrutiny when beginning to pray in earnest, responding to prayer with a life of conversion.

* * *

"I've no desire to change my ministry because I love it! I feel like writing is a vocation within a vocation. And I'd be happy to stay at America Media until I die," Jim recently told me.[12]

The first talk he gave on the subject of Lazarus—who is one of only two people in the gospels whom it says Jesus especially loved—was at the Los Angeles Religious Education Congress, at the Anaheim Convention Center, in early 2019. Lazarus is the subject of his next planned book.

Nineteen years earlier, when Jim received his first invitation to speak at LA Congress, an annual gathering in the Archdiocese of Los Angeles of over thirty thousand Catholics, he actually turned them down. He was unfamiliar with the gathering and its importance in the religious world and was at the time loath to travel. His publisher at the time, Robert Ellsberg of Orbis Books, expressed dismay. "You turned them down!?" he said to Jim. "No one turns them down!" So several years later, in 2005, when Jim was invited to LA Congress the following spring, he knew better and quickly said yes. As of this writing, he hasn't missed a Congress since.

"The happiest place on earth," he called LA Congress at the beginning of that first talk in 2005 in the big arena. Congress takes place in the convention center almost directly across the street from a certain internationally renowned amusement park in Anaheim. So Jim added to his comment that Congress was the happiest place to be, saying: "Not Disneyland. Because we have the Real Presence here, and they do not," to many laughs.[13]

The Religious Education Congress was only one of many speaking engagements that has increasingly filled Jim's already busy calendar of writing, continuing his regular priestly ministerial duties, and participating in the ordinary daily life of his local Jesuit community. (In 2015, America Media sold its longtime headquarters in Midtown Manhattan for a tidy sum, thus separating the offices from the Jesuit community. The new Jesuit community, which continues to be called America House, and where Jim also moved, was relocated to the Upper West Side of Manhattan, across the street from Fordham's Lincoln Center Campus.)

The invitations began coming in earnest following the publication of *My Life with the Saints* in 2006. In the years since, a sizeable number of weekday nights and weekends find Jim traveling to Catholic parishes, colleges and universities, retreat centers and conferences mainly in the Northeastern United States but sometimes farther afield. (Lately he's also been speaking to groups via Skype.) During every season of the year, and on topics as varied as Jesus, the saints, humor, prayer, and LGBT Catholics, he speaks to groups as small as parish book clubs and to gatherings as large as the LA Congress, where upwards of five thousand people gather for a talk.

His interest in Lazarus was sparked by personal experience. This is where his writing always seems to begin. One year, during his annual retreat, Jim mentioned struggles he was having letting go of certain qualities (needing to be liked, needing to control things, negative thinking), to become who he truly wanted to become. His spiritual director suggested that he pray with the story of Lazarus. He did, and he found he was being invited to let these things "die" in him.

In his talk at LA Congress, Jim began by describing how easy it was, in the time of Jesus, to walk from Jerusalem, over the Mount of Olives, to Bethany where Lazarus lived with his sisters Mary and Martha. Today, since the Israeli government built a wall to separate Palestinian territory, this is no longer possible. The Palestinians call the town, not Bethany, but El-Azariyeh, which in Arabic means "the place of Lazarus." Jim then told the story of Jesus' friendship with Lazarus and his sisters, the death of the man who was enigmatic in Jesus' circle (and perhaps a man who was somehow disabled, as Jean Vanier, the late founder of the L'Arche communities, suggested in his writings), and the way that

Martha scolded Jesus for not coming earlier to Bethany to keep her brother from dying. "He should have prevented suffering. It's easy to agree with her," he said.

"From time to time we need to ask ourselves, 'What part of me needs to die?'" Jim continued. He went on to describe what happened in his Ignatian practice of contemplation, placing himself in the gospel story, during that retreat. He'd imagined himself in the tomb as Lazarus. He'd listened for God's voice, and then he encouraged his listeners to do the same. "For me, Lazarus's tomb, the physical place and the spiritual place in my prayer, became the place to leave behind what I no longer needed, whatever was keeping me from new life. . . . I imagined I heard Jesus's voice calling to the parts of me that wanted to live," he said.

This is a good indication of what Jim's Lazarus book might be about. As he recently explained to me: "For the last few years, the way I've decided what to write next is to notice what I'm attracted to, and to trust that it's the Holy Spirit that's pushing me in that direction. Nothing too mysterious or mystical about it, really."[14] There is also the way that Jim seems to use his own experience with God to suggest a process that is available to everyone.

"What do you want to leave behind in the tomb?" he told the audience that day at LA Congress.

Again, he was taking what he had learned from Ignatian tradition and practice and offering it to others. He hopes to do the same for the rest of his life.

Acknowledgments

A book like this has no collaborators but many people to thank. I will leave the notes to explain primarily who those people are.

To those who have written before about James Martin, to those who edited and published him, and to those who were willing to be interviewed, thank you. Most of all, to James Martin, who willingly answered all my queries, responded quickly to my many email interviews, and shared personal documents (including letters he had forgotten he had kept), thank you. Also, two long in-person interviews took place in March and May 2019, providing many of the insights in the book that are not noted with sources.

And thank you to my wife, Michal Woll, for her love, wisdom, good humor, and friendship.

This book is dedicated to my parents, who moved back to the Midwest, and with whom I spent many wonderful hours, during the time of writing. I am grateful to them for so many things.

Notes

Chapter One:
Plymouth Meeting, Wharton, General Electric—
pages 1–16

1. Email interview, January 25, 2019.

2. William J. Buck, *History of Montgomery County within the Schuylkill Valley* (Norristown, PA: E.L. Acker, 1859), 81.

3. James Martin, "Of Many Things," *America*, November 5, 2007, available online at https://www.americamagazine.org/issue/632/many -things/many-things.

4. *The Jesuit Guide*, 104.

5. *In Good Company*, 5.

6. *The Jesuit Guide*, 72.

7. Email interview, January 27, 2019.

8. James Martin, "Of Many Things," *America*, April 18, 2005.

9. "I was a distinctly uncurious person." Email interview, February 2, 2018; *In Good Company*, 14.

10. James Martin, "Francis, Superstar," *Philadelphia* magazine, September 2015, 88.

11. Martin, "Francis, Superstar," 88.

12. Email interview, January 24, 2019.

13. *In Good Company*, 17.

14. *In Good Company*, 18.

15. Email interview, April 11, 2019.

16. James Martin, "Television, Etc.: Everything Is Rosie," *America*, August 17, 1996, 24.

17. Email interview, January 25, 2019.

18. Christopher D. Brown, CFA, email interview, August 7, 2018.

19. James Martin, in Judy Baca, "Finding Wealth in Priestly Poverty," *Times Herald*, Swarthmore, PA, May 29, 2001, D2.

20. Letter, to Eleanor S. Martin, September 5, 1988.

21. Email interview, April 11, 2019.

22. James Martin, commencement address, May 12, 2018, Loyola University New Orleans, transcribed from the video available at https://www.youtube.com/watch?v=WkqdWMosDHU.

Chapter Two:
Varieties of Spiritual Formation—pages 17–55

1. Eleanor Spano Martin, email interview, May 7, 2019.

2. Carolyn Martin Buscarino, email interview, May 13, 2019.

3. This story is told in *In Good Company*, 74.

4. *The Jesuit Guide*, 6.

5. Letters, to Eleanor S. Martin, September 5, 1988, and September 12, 1988.

6. William Campbell, SJ, written interview, March 11, 2019.

7. All quotes and references to *In Good Company*, 4.

8. Letter, to Eleanor Martin, October 30, 1988.

9. Letter, to Eleanor Martin, March 3, 1989.

10. Letter, to Eleanor Martin, April 30, 1989.

11. *My Life with the Saints*, 277.

12. Email interview, June 13, 2019.

13. *My Life with the Saints*, 278.

14. James Martin, "Hope in Loneliness," *Review for Religious* 52, no. 2 (March–April 1993): 236.

15. Letter, faxed to Mr. and Mrs. James Martin, August 20, 1992.

16. James Martin, "Who Cares about Africa?," *Consolata Missionaries Magazine*, July–August 1995, 12.

17. *A Jesuit Off-Broadway*, 101.

18. Letter, to Mr. and Mrs. James Martin, September 11, 1992.

19. James Martin, "Rescuing St. Al," *National Jesuit News*, December 1992/January 1993, 20.

20. Letter, to the Martins, February 11, 1993.

21. Email interview, July 15, 2018.

22. Cassette tape, recorded January 17, 1993.

23. *A Jesuit Off-Broadway*, 178.

24. Letter, to the Martins, March 12, 1993.

25. Letter, to the Martins, June 5, 1993.

26. James Martin, "Of Many Things," *America*, May 20, 2000, 2.

27. Alyson Krueger, "Bless Me, Father, For I Have Published," *Pennsylvania Gazette*, March/April 2012, 58.

28. Email interview, April 11, 2019.

29. Email interview, April 28, 2019.

30. Martin, "Of Many Things," May 20, 2000, 2.

31. *This Our Exile*, 211.

32. Letter, to Mom and Dad and C and C, August 26, 1992.

33. Email interview, July 15, 2018.

34. James Martin, "Television, Etc.: Journeys Sacred and Profane," *America*, December 17, 1994, 22.

35. Rev. Leonard F. Villa and Maria del Carmen Tapia, letters, *America*, March 25, 1995, 27–29.

36. William Schmitt, letters, *America*, April 1, 1995, 28.

37. Mark Raper, SJ, from James Martin, "Television, Etc.: Seeking the Sources of Hope; An Interview with Mark Raper," *America*, March 25, 1995, 12. Then, James Martin, "Who Cares about Africa?," *America*, May 13, 1995, 16–20. And anonymous quote from James Martin, "Television, Etc.: Communicable Diseases," *America*, June 3, 1995, 25.

38. Thomas J. Reese, SJ, email interview, July 27, 2018.

39. James Martin, "Meta-Coverage," *America*, March 4, 1995, 25.

40. James Martin, "Chefs, Cheetahs, and Martha Stewart," *Catholic Digest*, April 1997, 60–62.

41. James Martin, "Collared," *America*, March 2, 1996, 9–10.

42. James Martin, "Television, Etc.: Learning and Unlearning," *America*, November 20, 1996, 23.

43. James Martin, "The Rich Are Different," *America*, January 27, 1996, 22–23.

44. James Martin, "Television, Etc.: Computer Network," *America*, September 14, 1996, 26.

45. James Martin, "Television, Etc.: Coarse TV," *America*, September 16, 2000, 31.

46. Paula Fitzgerald, email interview, August 6, 2018.

47. Advent reflection published on Facebook, November 27, 2011. Still available at https://www.facebook.com/notes/fr-james-martin-sj /advent-the-season-of-desire/10150389836004538/.

48. *The Jesuit Guide*, 60–61.

49. James Martin, "How Can I Find God?," *America*, September 30, 1995, 12–21.

50. Joseph Bernardin, in "How Can I Find God?," *America*, February 15, 1997.

51. Email interview, July 26, 2018.

52. James Martin, "How Can I Find God? Another Look," *America*, August 30–September 6, 1997, 11–17.

53. James Martin, "Television, Etc.: Thinking Differently," *America*, January 3, 1998, 22.

54. James Martin, "Of Many Things," *America*, May 8, 1999, 2.

55. James Martin, "Television, Etc.: A Tale of Three Cities," *America*, May 2, 1998, 21.

56. James Martin, "Of Many Things," *America*, October 17, 1998, 2. Thomas J. Reese, SJ, was the new editor in chief at the magazine, and he often offered the "Of Many Things" front page to Martin.

57. William A. Donohue, letters, *America*, October 24, 1998, 30.

58. James Martin, "Of Many Things," *America*, January 16–23, 1999, 2.

59. *A Jesuit Off-Broadway*, 159.

60. James Martin, "Of Many Things," *America*, November 14, 1998, 2.

61. James Martin, "Of Many Things," *America*, November 25, 2000, 2.

62. James Martin, "Of Many Things," *America*, October 9, 1999, 2.

63. James Martin, "Why I Am Pro-Life," *America*, January 10, 2019.

64. *America*, May 20, 2000, 25.

Chapter Three:
Journalism and Vocation—pages 56–73

1. James Martin, "Television, Etc.: The Year in TV," *America*, July 15–22, 2000, 21.

2. *America*, January 15–22, 2000, cover.

3. James Martin, "Anti-Catholicism in the United States: The Last Acceptable Prejudice?," *America*, March 25, 2000, 8–16, 10.

4. William A. Donohue, letters, *America*, April 8, 2000, 44.

5. *The Jesuit Guide*, 79, 80.

6. James Martin, "September 10, 2001 . . . The Day Before," *New York Observer*, December 17, 2001, 25.

7. Email interview, July 13, 2018.

8. Thomas J. Reese, SJ, email interview, July 27, 2018.

9. James Martin, interview with Ed Thompson, October 15, 2001, for the *September 11, 2001 Oral History Narrative and Memory Project*, Columbia University Oral History Research Office.

10. James Martin, interview with Peter McDermott, "God Amid the Suffering," *Irish Echo*, March 13–19, 2002, 58.

11. James Martin, "A Prayer at Ground Zero," transcript of video published August 22, 2011, by *America* magazine on YouTube, available at https://www.youtube.com/watch?v=Jdra46PYovc.

12. Headlines from "Signs of the Times," *America*, October 1, 2001, 4–5. Then, James Martin, "The Laying Down of Life," *America*, October 1, 2001, 7–9.

13. Martin, "The Laying Down of Life," 9.

14. CNN Saturday Edition broadcast, official transcript, March 30, 2002.

15. Bob Minzesheimer, " 'Searching for God' Offers Spiritual Look at Ground Zero," *USA Today*, September 19, 2002, 7D.

16. Terry Golway, "A Priest's Search at Ground Zero," *New York Observer*, September 16, 2002.

17. *In Good Company*, x.

18. Email interview, November 30, 2017.

19. Email interview, November 30, 2017.

20. From "When Your Pastor Is a CPA," by Elizabeth Bernstein, *Wall Street Journal*, October 19, 2001, W6, W8.

21. James Martin, quoted in "From HR Hotshot to Jesuit Priest," *Workforce*, November 2001, 15.

22. Retta Blaney, "Jesuitry at GE?," *Wall Street Journal Sunday*, April 8, 2001, F1.

23. The Rev. James Martin, "The Confessions of a New Priest," *Philadelphia Inquirer*, May 27, 2001, B5. Thomas Merton, *The Sign of Jonas* (New York: Harvest, 1981), 181.

24. James Martin, "Television, Etc.: Contemplation in Action," *America*, April 8, 1995, 21.

25. James Martin, "Of Many Things," *America*, December 21–28, 2009.

26. Thomas J. Reese, SJ, email interview, July 27, 2018.

27. Email interview, December 17, 2017.

28. James Martin, "Choosing Celibacy," *New York Times*, March 25, 2002, A21.

29. Garry Wills, "The Case Against Celibacy," *The Boston Globe Magazine*, March 24, 2002, 22, 24.

30. "Silent No Longer: A Gay Priest Speaks Out (Final Part in a Series)," interview by Bill McGarvey and Mike Hayes, February 25, 2005, www.bustedhalo.com/dimensions/features63.htm.

31. Vatican Congregation for Catholic Education, Cardinal Zenon Grocholewski, prefect, "Instruction Concerning the Criteria for the Discernment of Vocations with Regard to Persons with Homosexual Tendencies in View of Their Admission to the Seminary and to Holy Orders," available at http://www.vatican.va/roman_curia/congregations /ccatheduc/documents/rc_con_ccatheduc_doc_20051104_istruzione _en.html.

32. James Martin, "'The Passion': If Only Gibson Had Shown the Death and the Life," *Newsday*, February 25, 2004.

33. James Martin, "Keating Leaves a Catholic Laity in Limbo," *Newsday*, June 19, 2003, A31.

34. James Martin, "Keeping the Collar through the Crisis," *Sun*, March 8, 2004, 15A.

Chapter Four:
Looking to the Saints—pages 74–85

1. James Martin, "Hope in Loneliness," 237.

2. James Martin, "Rescuing St. Al," *Catholic Digest*, May 1993, 20, 24.

3. James Martin, written interview, March 17, 2019.

4. *My Life with the Saints*, 5.

5. James Martin, "Priest Lets Friend Choose His Sacrifice for Lent," NPR's *All Things Considered*, interview with Melissa Block, February 28, 2006.

6. James Martin, "Trials of the Saints," *New York Times*, March 3, 2008, A25; "His Wife's a Saint So Is Her Husband," *Wall Street Journal*, W11; "The Hidden Man of Christmas," *Slate Magazine*, online, December 23, 2008.

7. Kelly Hughes, email interview, February 6, 2019.

8. James Martin, "Speaking Up," *O, The Oprah Magazine*, October 2010, 208; and Letters, *New York Times Book Review*, January 18, 2009, 4.

9. Email interview, April 11, 2019.

10. Letter, to Thomas J. Regan, SJ, November 5, 2008.

Chapter Five:
Going to the Theater—pages 86–94

1. James Martin, "Of Many Things," *America*, February 12, 2000, 2.

2. James Martin, "The Last Acceptable Prejudice?," *America*, March 25, 2000, 13.

3. Martin, "The Last Acceptable Prejudice?," 8.

4. From the foreword to *A Jesuit Off-Broadway*, xi.

5. *A Jesuit Off-Broadway*, xi.

6. *A Jesuit Off-Broadway*, 45.

7. Quoted in Jason Zinoman, "Hell to Pay: Stephen Adly Guirgis and a Priestly Advisor Love the Sinner in *The Last Days of Judas Iscariot*," *Time Out New York*, February 17–23, 2005, 127.

8. James Martin, quoted in "A Priest Remembers Philip Seymour Hoffman, James Martin, S.J., Recalls Working with Actor on 'Doubt,' 'Judas Iscariot,'" *Huffington Post*, February 3, 2014, https://www.huffpost.com/entry/james-martin-philip-seymour-hoffman_n_4717228.

9. From Julie L. Rattey, "Q&A: Father Jim Martin, SJ," *Catholic Digest*, December 2008, 31.

10. Thomas J. Reese, SJ, email interview, July 27, 2018.

11. Email interview, January 28, 2019.

12. "Editor of Jesuit Magazine Resigns Under Pressure," *Los Angeles Times*, May 7, 2005.

13. James Martin, "Of Many Things," *America*, June 20, 2005.

14. Email interview, January 28, 2019.

15. *Celebrating Good Liturgy*, xv.

Chapter Six:
More Bad Priests, Ignatian Practices, and Joy— pages 95–108

1. James Martin, "Television, Etc.: Celibacy and Sound Bites," *America*, May 6, 1995, 24. The film was called *Priest*.

2. James Martin, "The Church and the Homosexual Priest: Facing the Challenges and Accepting the Gifts Offered by Homosexual Priests in the Catholic Church," *America*, November 4, 2000, 11–15.

3. James Martin, "Choosing Celibacy," *New York Times*, March 25, 2002, https://www.nytimes.com/2002/03/25/opinion/choosing-celibacy.html.

4. James Martin, tweet, Friday morning, March 16, 2018.

5. *The Jesuit Guide*, 211.

6. Martin, "Choosing Celibacy," A21.

7. *The Jesuit Guide*, 85.

8. William Campbell, SJ, written interview, March 11, 2019.

9. Email interview, December 27, 2017.

10. James Martin, "Shadows in Prayer: The Seven D's of the Spiritual Life," *America*, March 17, 2008, 21.

11. James Martin, "Television, Etc.: Sister Act," *America*, September 20, 1997, 28.

12. James Martin, "Television, Etc.: Good News!," *America*, February 14, 1998, 26. The context, here, was a review of the new PBS show *Religion and Ethics Newsweekly*, hosted by Bob Abernethy.

13. All quotes from the Mother Angelica article are from James Martin, "Television, Etc.: Mater et Magistra," *America*, August 12, 1995, 32–33.

14. James Martin, "The Most Infallible Sign: Recovering Joy, Humor and Laughter in the Spiritual Life," *America*, April 2, 2007, 15; and *Between Heaven and Mirth*, 52.

15. Lane Lambert, "The Saints Laughed, Too," *Patriot Ledger*, August 22, 2008.

16. James Martin, "Scripting the Saints: Reflections by Four Distinguished Authors," *American Catholic Studies* 122, no. 3 (2011): 64–65.

17. Email interview, December 30, 2017.

Chapter Seven:
A Life with Jesus—pages 109–23

1. James Martin, "Frustrations—Jesus' Ministry and Ours," *Review for Religious* 52, no. 6 (November–December 1993): 870, 872.

2. This quote, and the one before it, are from a written interview, December 20, 2017.

3. James Martin, "Daniel J. Harrington, SJ, RIP," *America*, February 8, 2014, https://www.americamagazine.org/content/all-things /daniel-j-harrington-sj-rip.

4. *Jesus: A Pilgrimage*, 410, 415.

5. All of these quotes are from Father James Martin, "The Life of a Jesuit," in *Pope for a New World*, by Howard Chua-Eoan and *Time* contributors (New York: Time, 2013), 28–31.

6. For the original account of Martin suggesting the interview, see Matt Malone, SJ, "Of Many Things," September 17, 2013, https:// www.americamagazine.org/issue/many-things-26. The book: *A Big Heart Open to God: A Conversation with Pope Francis*, interview by Antonio Spadaro, SJ, spiritual reflections by James Martin, SJ, foreword by Matt Malone, SJ (New York: HarperOne, 2013).

7. "Contents," *Philadelphia* magazine, September 2015, 5.

8. James Martin, "Television, Etc.: The Gospel According to Block-buster," *America*, May 3, 1997, 22.

9. Email interview, April 11, 2019.

10. Martin, from an interview with Ines San Martin, "Jesuit James Martin Says New Scorsese Movie Is 'Like a Prayer,' " *Crux*, December 7, 2016, https://cruxnow.com/interviews/2016/12/07/father-james-martin-on-movie-silence/.

11. Brendan Busse, SJ, "Andrew Garfield Played a Jesuit in Silence, but He Didn't Expect to Fall in Love with Jesus," *America,* January 23, 2017.

12. *Seven Last Words*, 118.

13. Email interview, February 11, 2018.

14. *A Jesuit Off-Broadway*, 49.

15. Ron Hansen, email interview, January 18, 2018.

16. *The Jesuit Guide*, 68.

17. Mary Karr, telephone interview, February 3, 2019.

Chapter Eight:
Reaching Out to the Margins—pages 124–48

1. Transcribed from "Civility in America, Part I—Religion," a public conversation with Ross Douthat at the Sheen Center in New York City, December 13, 2017, https://www.youtube.com/watch?v=ikNLBvAxqk0.

2. Email interview, January 27, 2019.

3. Jim Russell, "The Insanely Stupid 'LGBT' Rhetoric of Fr. James Martin," ChurchMilitant.com, February 5, 2019.

4. Frank Bruni, "The Scariest Catholic in America," *New York Times*, February 3, 2018.

5. James Alison, "Homosexuality in the Clergy: Caught in a Trap of Dishonesty," *The Tablet*, August 1, 2018, http://www.thetablet.co.uk/features/2/14068/homosexuality-among-the-clergy-caught-in-a-trap-of-dishonesty.

6. James Martin, "The Virtues of Catholic Anger," *New York Times*, August 15, 2018, https://www.nytimes.com/2018/08/15/opinion/the-virtues-of-catholic-anger.html.

7. See "The Causes and Context of Sexual Abuse of Minors by Catholic Priests in the United States, 1950–2010," a report presented to the United States Conference of Catholic Bishops by the John Jay College Research Team, May 2011, available at usccb.org.

8. Andrew Sullivan, "Cleansing the Catholic Church of Its Sins," *New York Magazine*, August 17, 2018, available at http://nymag .com/daily/intelligencer/2018/08/cleansing-the-catholic-church-of-its -sins.html.

9. James Martin, tweet, 11:08 a.m., August 19, 2018.

10. James Martin, "The Witch Hunt for Gay Priests," August 30, 2018, available at https://www.americamagazine.org/faith/2018/08/30 /witch-hunt-gay-priests.

11. Quoted in Cindy Wooden, "Archbishop Chaput Urges Synod to Use Care with Language, Especially on Sexuality," *Catholic News Service*, October 4, 2018.

12. David Gibson, "Vatican Bishops at Synod Struggle with What to Call Gay People," *Religion News Service*, October 23, 2018.

13. Transcribed from video: James Martin, SJ, "Faith in Focus," November 15, 2018, https://www.youtube.com/watch?v=DDDCQIa EsHE.

14. Pope Francis, quoted in Rose Gamble, "Gay Priests Must Be 'Impeccably Responsible' Says Pope," *The Tablet*, December 3, 2018.

15. Email interview, April 11, 2019.

16. James Martin, "Building a Bridge: Catholic Church and LGBT Community," published by Villanova University on September 6, 2017, available at https://www.youtube.com/watch?v=TNEt2kK60VM.

17. Transcribed from "Civility in America, Part I—Religion."

18. James Martin, "Help Wanted: A Prayer for Frustrated Catholics," *America*, August 13–20, 2012, 26.

19. James Martin, "Television, Etc.: Contemplation in Action," *America*, April 8, 1995, 21.

20. James Martin, "Television, Etc.: Random February Thoughts," *America*, February 15, 1997, 29.

21. Amazon reader reviews signed by Anonymous, Rich Leonardi, and J. Sullivan, as seen on the book detail page for *Building a Bridge* on July 5, 2018.

22. Matthew Schmitz @matthewschmitz, tweet, 5:03 p.m., July 20, 2018.

23. James Martin, tweets, 8:17 p.m.–8:21 p.m., July 20, 2018.

24. Email interview, April 28, 2019.

25. Email interview, April 28, 2019.

26. Email interview, April 28, 2019.

27. Nielsen BookScan numbers recorded as of July 23, 2018. The *My Life with the Saints* breakdown was as follows: hardcover, 22,379; paperback, 93,114; tenth anniversary paperback, 3,269.

28. Telephone interview with Michael Maudlin, July 23, 2018.

29. Email interview, May 23, 2018. "It's just a coincidence. The gay comment came out of the controversy surrounding the Chilean bishops, not in response to anything I've written! I met him once after a Mass, but really just to shake hands for a second. I'm trying to get a copy of my book to him."

30. Robert W. McElroy, "Attacks on James Martin Expose a Cancer within the U.S. Catholic Church," *America*, September 18, 2017.

31. Available at https://www.americamagazine.org/faith/2018 /06/11/father-james-martin-speak-welcoming-lgbt-catholics-world -meeting-families.

32. See, for example, http://catholicherald.co.uk/news/2018/08/13 /10000-sign-petition-to-stop-fr-james-martin-speaking-at-world -meeting-of-families/.

33. "Young People, the Faith and Vocational Discernment," Instrumentum Laboris for the Synod 2018, available at http://www.synod2018 .va/content/synod2018/en/fede-discernimento-vocazione/instrumentum -laboris-for-the-synod-2018--young-people--the-faith.html.

34. David Gibson, tweet, 8:47 a.m., August 2, 2018.

Chapter Nine:
Priest in the Media—pages 149–58

1. James Martin, quoted in Michael Paulson, "O'Malley Encounters Obama at Funeral for Senator," *Boston Sunday Globe*, August 30, 2009; and "Comedian Sarah Silverman: End World Hunger? Sell the Vatican," Associated Press, Rome, October 16, 2009.

2. "An Election Day Prayer from Father James Martin," *America* online, November 8, 2016, https://www.americamagazine.org/faith /2016/11/08/election-day-prayer-father-james-martin.

3. James Martin, "Television, Etc.: You Shall Not Oppress an Alien," *America*, December 14, 1996, 25. Then, "Reverend Jim Martin Discusses the Moral Imperative to Welcome Migrant Children, Op-Ed," *NowThis News*, published on YouTube, July 14, 2018, https://www.youtube.com/watch?v=kNzXKYqYZWI.

4. James Martin, "Why Did Judas Do It?," *America*, May 29, 2006, 15.

5. Email interview, December 15, 2017.

6. James Martin, "Saints or Assassins? Opus Dei and *The Da Vinci Code*," *America*, June 5–12, 2006, 10–11.

7. James Martin, "The Literal Flesh-and-Blood Resurrection Is the Heart of My Faith," *America*, April 23, 2019.

8. James Martin, "Understanding Desire," *America* online, September 11, 2018.

9. Email interview with Evan Mascagni, April 16, 2019.

Chapter Ten:
Humility, Prayer, Lazarus—pages 159–69

1. "Fr. James Martin Answers 5 Common Questions about Silence," *America Media*, January 18, 2017, online at https://www.america magazine.org/arts-culture/2017/01/18/fr-james-martin-answers-5 -common-questions-about-silence.

2. James Martin, "Reflections on Chronic Illness and Pain, among Other Things," *America*, March 21, 1998.

3. James Martin, "Ploughing the Soul," *The Tablet*, March 1, 1997, 288.

4. James Martin, "Holy Dirt," *America*, February 25, 2008, 11.

5. Email interview, April 11, 2019.

6. James Martin, *Jesuitical* podcast, "LGBT Catholics Have Been Treated Like Dirt and We Can Do Better," June 16, 2017. Jim appears on the podcast at the 14:10 mark.

7. Email interview, January 3, 2018.

8. Martin, Facebook live, March 30, 2019. He couldn't be in South Bend for the ceremony and sent a video acceptance.

9. Most Reverend Jerome E. Listecki, "Archbishop Listecki in Response to Fr. Greg Greiten," December 19, 2017, available at https://www.archmil.org/News-2.0/Archbishop-Listecki-in-Response -to-Fr.-Greg-Greiten.htm.

10. Martin, *Jesuitical* podcast, "LGBT Catholics Have Been Treated Like Dirt," at 32:03.

11. Email interview, April 17, 2019.

12. Email interview, April 9, 2018.

13. March 23, 2019. As of this writing, the complete talk was available on YouTube at https://www.youtube.com/watch?v=V8OM0k YEHxQ.

14. Email interview, April 17, 2019.

Bibliography

Books by James Martin, SJ, referenced in the text and notes, by chronological order in which they were published:

(Editor) *How Can I Find God? The Famous and the Not-So-Famous Consider the Quintessential Question.* Liguori, MO: Liguori/Triumph, 1997.

This Our Exile: A Spiritual Journey with the Refugees of East Africa. Maryknoll, NY: Orbis Books, 1999.

In Good Company: The Fast Track from the Corporate World to Poverty, Chastity, and Obedience. New York: Sheed & Ward, 2000.

Searching for God at Ground Zero: A Memoir. New York: Sheed & Ward, 2002.

(Editor) *Awake My Soul: Contemporary Catholics on Traditional Devotions.* Chicago: Loyola Press, 2004.

(Editor) *Celebrating Good Liturgy: A Guide to the Ministries of the Mass.* Chicago: Loyola Press, 2005.

My Life with the Saints. Chicago: Loyola Press, 2006.

Lourdes Diary: Seven Days at the Grotto of Massabieille. Chicago: Loyola Press, 2006.

Becoming Who You Are: Insights on the True Self from Thomas Merton and Other Saints. Mahwah, NJ: Paulist Press, 2006.

A Jesuit Off-Broadway: Behind the Scenes with Faith, Doubt, Forgiveness, and More. Chicago: Loyola Press, 2007.

The Jesuit Guide to (Almost) Everything: A Spirituality for Real Life. New York: HarperOne, 2010.

Between Heaven and Mirth: Why Joy, Humor, and Laughter Are at the Heart of the Spiritual Life. New York: HarperOne, 2011.

Jesus: A Pilgrimage. New York: HarperOne, 2014.

The Abbey: A Story of Discovery. New York: HarperOne, 2015.

Seven Last Words: An Invitation to a Deeper Friendship with Jesus. New York: HarperOne, 2016.

Building a Bridge: How the Catholic Church and the LGBT Community Can Enter into a Relationship of Respect, Compassion, and Sensitivity. New York: HarperOne, 2017; 2nd ed., 2018.

Learning to Pray. New York: HarperOne, 2020.

Index